KS3 History

Third Edition

Renaissa
Revolut
Reformation

Britain 1509-1745

Aaron Wilkes

OXFORD
UNIVERSITY PRESS

Contents

Chapter 6:
Exit the Tudors, enter the Stuarts

Chapter 7:
England at war

Chapter 8:
Cromwell's Commonwealth

Chapter 9:
The Restoration

Chapter 10:
Who rules?

Chapter 11:
How did Britain change?

Introducing KS3 History

Thinking about History

Before exploring this book, take a few minutes to think about these questions.

- What do you think history is?

- What have you learned in History lessons before? Did you enjoy the lessons or not? Think about why that is.

- Have you read any books about things that happened a long time ago? Have you watched any television programmes, films or plays about past events? Which ones?

So what is history?

History is about what happened in the past. It's about people in the past, what they did and why they did it, what they thought, and what they felt. To enjoy history you need to have a good imagination. You need to be able to imagine what life was like long ago, or what it may have been like to be involved in past events.

What about my History lessons?

Your lessons are designed to show you how, why and when things have changed through time. For example, in the year this book starts (1509) the English king had lots of power and ruled over Wales and large parts of Ireland too… but not Scotland. He had to consult Parliament if he wanted to introduce new laws or raise taxes, but the king was still an incredibly powerful person. However, by this time this book ends (in 1745) there was one monarch who ruled over England, Wales, Ireland AND Scotland… a United Kingdom. And he was from Germany! Parliament was also much more powerful than it had ever been before.

So you must be wondering how these things changed, and why they changed, and when. This book will take you on that journey of discovery… and hopefully turn you into a top historian on the way!

How does this book fit in?

This book will get you thinking. You will be asked to look at different pieces of evidence and to try to work things out for yourself. Sometimes, two pieces of evidence about the same event won't agree with each other. You might be asked to think of reasons why that is. Your answers might not be the same as your friend's or even your teacher's answers. The important thing is to give **reasons** for your thoughts and ideas.

How to use this book

Features of the *Student Book*, are explained here and on the opposite page.

Key to icons

| Source bank | Film | Worksheet | History skills activity | Literacy | Numeracy |

Depth Study

In each book, there is a mini depth study that focuses on a significant event or concept. These sections give you the chance to extend and deepen your understanding of key moments in history.

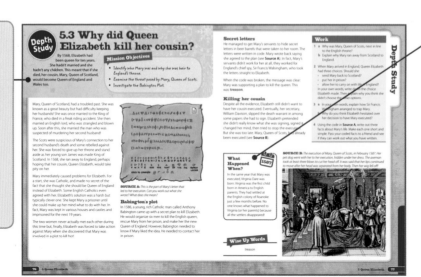

History skills

Be a Top Historian

Sometimes the tasks, ideas and sources will challenge you to think and act like a top historian and stretch your skills and abilities.

What Happened When?

This gives you an idea of what else is going on in the world (perhaps in another country on a different continent) at the same sort of time as the period you are studying in the lesson. It could also focus on a specific topic and make links across time, showing how things are connected.

Mission Objectives

All lessons in this book start by setting you 'Mission Objectives'. These are your key aims that set out your learning targets for the work ahead. At the end of the each lesson you should review these objectives and assess how well you've done.

Wise Up Words

Wise Up Words are the really important key words and terms that are vital to help you understand the topics. You can spot them easily because they are in **bold red** type. Look up their meanings in a dictionary or use the glossary at the back of the book. The glossary is a list of these words and their meanings.

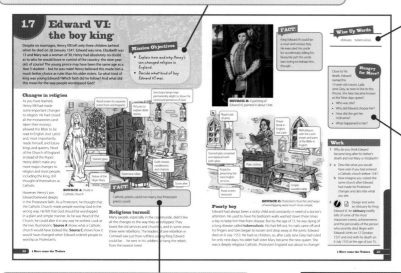

Hungry for More?

You might be asked to extend your knowledge and research beyond the classroom. This is a time to take responsibility for your own learning. You might be asked to research something in the library or on the Internet, work on a presentation, or design and make something. Can you meet the challenge?

Fact!

These are the funny, fascinating and amazing little bits of history that you don't usually get to hear about! But in this series, we think they're just as important – they give you insights into topics that you'll easily remember.

History Mystery

These sections give you an opportunity to pull all your skills together and investigate a controversial, challenging or intriguing aspect of the period, such as how the *Mary Rose* sank or whether the gunpowder plotters were framed.

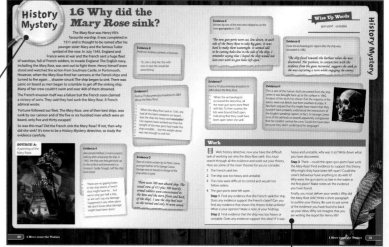

Work

Work sections are your opportunity to demonstrate your knowledge and understanding. You might be asked to:

- put events in chronological order
- explain how and why things changed over time
- work out why two people have different views about the same event
- discover what triggered an event… and uncover the consequences.

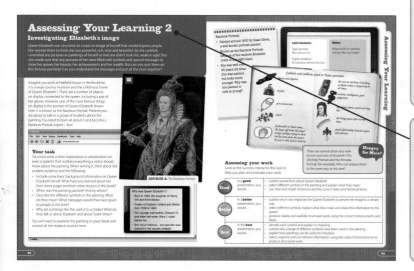

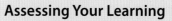

Assessing Your Learning

In the book, there are three extended assessments. These are opportunities for you to showcase what you have learned about the topic and to put your research and analysis skills to the test. Some are more creative, while some will focus on extended writing or looking at sources.

A journey through time from 1509 to 1745

This book covers the years 1509 to 1745: the time of the Tudors, the Stuarts… and the beginning of the Georgian period. Some of the world's most famous people lived at this time and some of history's most remembered events took place. This book highlights these memorable people and events as it takes you on a journey through this remarkable time. The period from 1509 to 1745 was one of great, and lasting, changes too, particularly in relation to religion and the power of Parliament. And many people's views of the world changed dramatically as explorers and traders discovered new routes to new lands, and new ideas and inventions changed the way people did things.

The timeline on these pages picks out some of these big events, well-known people, new ideas, changes and discoveries. Read it carefully!

1485

Henry Tudor becomes the first Tudor king – Henry VII

Guy Fawkes and the gunpowder plotters try to blow up Parliament

1603

James VI of Scotland becomes James I of England too and unites the two kingdoms

1605

1607

First successful English settlement is set up in North America

1642

English Civil War begins

Act of Union between England and Scotland; one Parliament in London runs both countries

The last Stuart, Queen Anne, dies, the throne passes to her nearest Protestant relation, who becomes George I; and so the Georgian era begins

1707

1688

The Glorious Revolution: James II is replaced by King William and Queen Mary

1714

1689

1665

The Great Plague

1666

Great Fire of London

English Bill of Rights: all monarchs, who must be Protestant, to rule in partnership with Parliament

1509

Henry VII dies and his son, Henry VIII, becomes king

1534

Henry VIII forms an independent Church of England

1558

Elizabeth I begins her 44-year reign

English trading in India begins

1600

1591

First performance of a play by William Shakespeare

The English defeat the Spanish Armada

1588

1562

England becomes involved in the African slave trade

1649

Charles I is executed

1649–1650

Cromwell's conquest of Ireland

1660

Restoration of the monarchy under Charles II

1649–1660

Parliament, followed by Oliver Cromwell, rules instead of a monarch

Work

1 **a** How do the Tudor, Stuart and Georgian periods of history get their names?

b Have you studied any of these periods of history before? If so, make a list of the events and people you can remember. If not, look through the timeline and list the people and events you have heard of before.

2 Finding out which year is in which century can be difficult. The easiest way is to cover up the last two numbers in the year and add one to the first two numbers. For example, 1562 is in the sixteenth century (cover up the 62 and add 1 to 15 to make 16!).

a Which century are the following years in?
 i 1649   **iii** 1665
 ii 1707   **iv** 1558

b Which century were each of the following events in?
 i The Glorious Revolution
 ii The Great Fire of London
 iii First performance of a Shakespeare play
 iv Death of Henry VII
 v James I unites Scotland and England

c Now put the five events above in the correct chronological order (the order in which they happened, from first to last).

1.1A What was Britain like in 1509?

This book is about the people and events of Britain between 1509 and 1745, a time of great change. For you to see how important these changes were, you must first find out about Britain in 1509. Then, towards the end of this book, you will be asked to compare the Britain of 1509 with the Britain of 1745.

Mission Objectives

- Examine what Britain was like in 1509.
- Summarize England's relationship with its neighbouring countries.
- Contrast Britain in 1509 with Britain today.

I am King Henry VIII. My father, Henry VII, was the first Tudor monarch. He ruled for over 20 years and has just died. He left me in charge of a peaceful country with plenty of money.

King Henry VIII

A baron

England and Scotland are separate countries. The English and the Scots have fought a lot over the years. I think of the English as the 'old enemy' and truly hate them! There are about half a million Scots.

Like most of the population, we are poor and live in the countryside. Some of the land is used for growing crops or grazing sheep, but most is woodland or wasteland. We live on what we grow. If we grow more than we need, we sell it at the local market in the nearest town. Most towns are still quite small but a few are growing fast. Only 10 per cent of people live in the towns. There are about 2 million people who live in England now.

I am King Henry's new wife. My name is Catherine and I'm a princess from an area called Aragon in Spain. I was once married to Henry's older brother Arthur... but Arthur died several years ago.

We lords and barons are rich and powerful. We own lots of land and sometimes help the king to make decisions. Most of us aim to work with the new king rather than against such a rich and powerful man.

Catherine of Aragon

A Scotsman

There is only one religion in Britain — Christianity. The Head of the Church is the Pope, who lives in Rome. Religion is a very important part of people's lives.

A villager

Over the years, English kings have tried to control us but have failed. They have only managed to control part of this country. About 800,000 people live here.

A priest

We politicians are very busy. We pass laws and collect taxes. In fact, the king must get our agreement if he wants any tax money, so we can be quite powerful at times!

The English control most of Wales but some areas are still run by independent Welsh princes like me. There are only about 200,000 people in Wales.

I am a student at the University of Oxford. We live in exciting times. New printed books spread ideas about art, medicine and religion. Some of the ideas of the ancient Greeks and Romans have been published too... and are fascinating us all!

An Irish chief

A Welshman

A student

A politician

Map (SOURCE A)

Scotland had been ruled by the Stuart family since 1371 and James IV ruled from 1488

SCOTLAND

IRELAND

WALES

ENGLAND
England was ruled by a king – Henry VIII

Wales had been conquered by England

Calais was the only part of France still ruled by England

Key

- English land ruled by the English king
- Irish land ruled by English lords, with English laws
- Irish land ruled mostly by the English king, with Irish laws
- Welsh land ruled mostly by the English king, with Welsh laws
- Welsh land ruled by the English Prince of Wales, with English laws
- Scotland – an independent country from England

SOURCE A: *Britain in 1509. England's king, Henry VIII was known as King of England, Lord of Ireland and Prince of Wales.*

Wise Up Words

independent   population

Work

1 Write out the paragraph below, choosing one answer from each pair of brackets.

In 1509, the King of England was (Henry VII/Henry VIII). He also controlled most of (Wales/Scotland) and part of Ireland. (Wales/Scotland) was an independent country. Some land was used for (fishing/farming) but most of it was wasteland or (woodland/Disneyland). Nine out of (ten/nine) people lived in the (towns/countryside) and grew their own food. If they grew (more/less) than they needed, they might go and sell it at the local (supermarket/market).

2 Draw a bar chart to show the population of England, Scotland, Ireland and Wales in 1509. Make sure you add a title.

SOURCE B: *What was Britain like?*

KING AND PARLIAMENT
England and Scotland had their own kings

FOOD AND DRINK
British citizens had a basic diet

THE KNOWN WORLD
North and South America, Europe, the west coast of Africa, India and the east coast of China known to the Europeans

CLOTHING
Clothing was a sign of status, as it is today; only the very wealthy wore expensive fabrics

HOMES
The rich lived in strong, well-defended homes, the poor lived in small, thatched-roof cottages

Britain in 1509

TRANSPORT
The rich travelled on horseback and by cart; the poor walked! Roads were in very poor condition

COMMUNICATION
Mainly by word of mouth

RELIGION
One common religion – Christianity. The Pope in Rome was the Head of the Christian Catholic Church

FURNITURE
Solid and wooden, few chairs

Everyday life

The sources on these pages show you what life was like in the early 1500s. Look through them carefully.

SOURCE A: *Common industries in Britain in 1509. As you can see, cloth making was one of Britain's most important industries and nearly every town would have had a group of spinners, weavers and dyers.*

What Happened When?

1509

In 1509, the same year that Henry VIII became King of England, a German man called Peter Henlein invented an early version of the pocket watch. It was called the 'Nuremberg Egg' and was a small, drum-shaped object with an hour hand only.

FACT!

There were about 8 million sheep in Britain in the early 1500s and only about 3 million people! The sheep were kept mainly to supply the cloth industry.

SOURCE B: *This woodcut shows a weaver at his loom.*

SOURCE C: *A fete at Bermondsey, near London in the 1500s, showing townspeople of all classes of society.*

'There are old men living in my village who have noticed three things to be greatly changed. One is the many chimneys recently erected. The second is the beds. Their fathers used to sleep on straw on rough mats covered only with a sheet and a good round log under their heads. Pillows were only for women in childbed. The third is the change from wooden plates to pewter ones and from wooden spoons to silver or tin.'

▲ **SOURCE D:** *Written by William Harrison, who lived in Essex in the 1500s.*

Hungry for More?

Find out the populations of England, Scotland, Ireland and Wales today. Draw another bar chart using these figures. Underneath it, write a paragraph comparing the two bar charts.
- Does England still have the largest population in Britain?
- What is the second most populated country in Britain?

FACT!

The currency was pounds, shillings and pence. The '£' (a fancy L) was used for pound (from the Latin 'Libra') meaning a pound in weight, 's' was used for shilling (an ancient English value) and 'd' was used for penny (from the Latin 'denarius'). The penny was the basic unit of currency. Twelve pence made a shilling and 20 shillings made a pound, so there were 240 pence to the pound. In the early 1500s, a farm worker could make a shilling a day – and bread (the main food) cost half a penny per loaf.

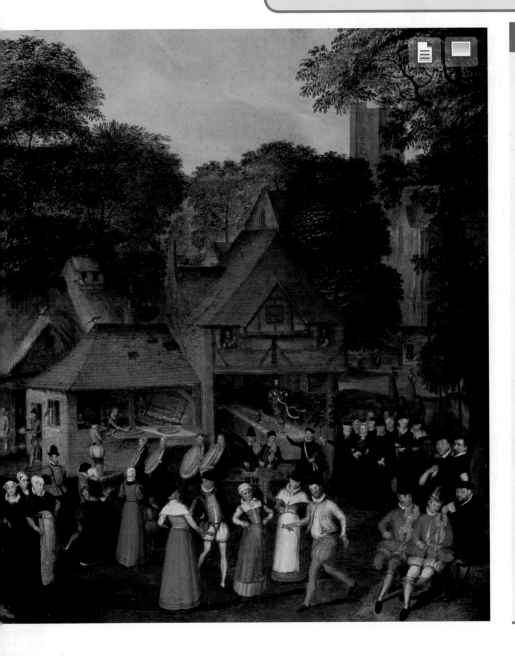

Work

1 Look at **Source C**.
   a Can you see:
      i the Tower of London in the background?
      ii two dogs fighting?
      iii four people holding large pies?
      iv two men playing violins?
      v a woman breastfeeding her baby?
   b What can you tell about life in the 1500s from this painting?

2 Look at **Source D**. According to the old men living in William Harrison's village in the 1500s, what were the three things that had changed most in recent times?

3 Divide a page into two columns. Write 'Britain in 1509' at the top of one column and 'Britain now' at the top of the other. List all the ways in which Britain in 1509 was different from Britain today. Choose what you think are the three most important differences and write a sentence or two explaining why you made your choices.

What was young Henry VIII like?

Everybody has heard of Henry VIII. Most people think they know a few things about him too. They usually say:

- He was a big fat bloke.
- He had six wives… or was it eight?
- He beheaded most of his wives.

Some of these statements are true. Henry did have six wives but he didn't chop the heads off most of them, although he did behead two! As for him being a big fat bloke – well yes, he was – but only for the last few years of his life. In fact, on his 45th birthday, Henry was the same size as he was when he became king!

Mission Objectives

- Examine how young Henry VIII spent his time and money.
- Judge how religious he was as a young man.

A new Tudor king

Henry's father, Henry VII, was unpopular towards the end of his reign because he taxed people heavily. When he died and Henry VIII became king in 1509, there were wild celebrations. The new king was tall, handsome and full of energy. The diagram on this page shows why many people thought he was ideally suited to be king.

Henry loved entertaining.

He enjoyed hunting.

FACT!

Henry VIII employed someone to wipe his bottom! He was officially called the Groom of the Stool. It was a much prized job because the employee got to spend so much time with the king!

Henry was a keen sportsman.

He loved jousting.

He was a keen poet.

He wrote music.

Bonjour!

Buenos días!

SOURCE A: *A portrait of Henry VIII showing him in his late twenties.*

He spoke four languages.

Henry the Great?

As you will learn, many fantastic facts surround the life of Henry VIII. For example, Henry was desperate to become known as a 'super king' and even liked to call himself 'Henry the Great'. But although he is most famous for his wives, the most important events in Henry's life were the religious changes he made. Not only did they affect religion in Henry's time, they changed religion in England and Wales for good.

Henry the good Catholic

Henry was a very religious man and, like most people in the country at the time, he was **Catholic**. He visited church at least three times a day and even wrote a book supporting the **Pope**, who was the Head of the Catholic Church. Henry was such a good Catholic that in 1521, the Pope rewarded him with the title *Fidei Defensor*, which means Defender of the Faith. Henry loved this title and was very proud of it – and so were many other kings and queens. You can still see the letters FD or 'Fid. Def.' on British coins today.

Wise Up Words

Catholic   excommunicate   Pope

It all goes wrong

However, by 1533, Henry had fallen out with the Pope, who **excommunicated** him, meaning he was expelled from the Catholic Church. This was a very serious punishment at the time because it meant that the person could not talk to a priest about their sins. If a priest did not forgive you for your sins, then you wouldn't get to heaven. So how did Henry VIII and the Pope fall out with each other? What had Henry done that was so terrible that he received the worst kind of religious punishment? The next few pages chart an amazing story.

FACT!

Henry loved to bet on anything – cards, dice, tennis, wrestling or jousting. He used to win (and lose) the equivalent of thousands of pounds every day. Henry also loved to dress in the smartest, most expensive clothes. His silk shirts, gold buttons and jewel-encrusted jackets would have cost a fortune. So, too, would his legendary parties, held at any of Henry's 55 palaces.

Work

 The Big Write!

Your task is to write a profile of the young King Henry VIII.

Search through the text to find out details about the young king, using the following subheadings to guide your writing:

- Henry the athlete
- Henry the good Catholic
- Henry the big spender.

Finally, write your own opinion in answer to the following question, 'Should the young King Henry have been called Henry the Great?'

SOURCE B: *Can you see 'F.D.' on this £1 coin?*

Henry VIII, his first wife and his big problem

Henry's problems with religion started with his love life. His first wife was a Spanish princess called Catherine of Aragon. He first met her in 1501 when she came to England to marry his big brother Arthur! So how did Henry end up marrying her? What problems did this cause? And what did his relationship with Catherine mean for the future of religion in England?

Mission Objectives

- *Explore how and why Henry VIII fell out with the Pope.*
- *Examine how this affected the life of Henry and religion in the whole of England.*

Henry marries his dead brother's wife!

A marriage between Prince Arthur and Princess Catherine would mean friendship between England and Spain. However, Arthur died only a year after the marriage. To avoid sending widow Catherine home to Spain and upsetting her father, Henry VII arranged for his second son, Henry, to marry her. The wedding took place in 1509, the same year that King Henry VII died. Seventeen-year-old Henry became King Henry VIII and Catherine of Aragon was his first queen.

Henry in love

Henry and Catherine were a popular and loving couple. In 1513, whilst Henry was in France, Catherine ran the country for him. Her army even beat a Scottish army at the Battle of Flodden. Catherine brought Henry a present home from the battle… the dead King of Scotland's coat, still stained with his blood!

Henry and Catherine were happily married for nearly 20 years. Henry once said, 'If I were still free, I would choose her for a wife above all others.' What a romantic man! But the marriage didn't last. As we all know, he had five more wives after Catherine… so what went wrong? Read through the cartoon carefully to discover why Henry and Catherine's marriage ended.

1 Henry desperately wanted a son.

 Catherine gave birth to six children, but only one, a girl called Mary, survived.

2 By 1527, Henry thought Catherine was too old to have any more children. Henry wanted to divorce Catherine. He'd fallen in love with another woman too – Anne Boleyn!

3 Henry got his lawyers to look secretly into whether his marriage to Catherine was legal or not.

The marriage was found to be legal – but Henry still wanted his divorce.

4 The Pope was the only man who could give Henry the divorce he wanted… but he refused!

Henry hated the fact that the Pope had this power over him… but he had a plan.

5 Henry ignored the Pope. He made himself Head of the Church of England instead of the Pope. The Pope was furious but Henry could do as he pleased.

Henry changes a nation

Henry's desire for a baby boy began a series of events that altered religion in England forever. In one move, he had his divorce and made himself more powerful. The Pope in Rome no longer had the English Church under his control – Henry did – and all its wealth too! To this day, the Head of the Church of England is the king or queen.

Yet despite this change of Church leader and the closing of the monasteries, Henry only really made one other major religious change. From 1538, he ordered that every church must have an English copy of the Bible. At last, ordinary people could understand what their religion was teaching them.

Wise Up Words

Dissolution   Reformation

FACT!

Historians like to give titles to major historical changes! Henry's changes to the Church are known as the English '**Reformation**' because Henry was reforming (another word for changing) the English Church.
When he closed down the monasteries, it was known as the '**Dissolution**' of the monasteries. Dissolution is another word for breaking up.

---

6 In early 1533, Henry gave himself the divorce he desired.

Henry could now marry Anne Boleyn.

7 Henry married his second wife, Anne Boleyn, in 1533. She was already pregnant.

Anne gave birth to a girl, Elizabeth, in September 1533. Henry was very disappointed. Why?

8 Some of the monks in England didn't support Henry's new Church of England. They supported the Pope.

So he closed down all the monasteries and the land was sold.

9 The monasteries were very wealthy and the king made a good profit.

But the Pope was furious again. Not only had Henry ignored him and closed all of the Catholic monasteries in England, but he had now stolen all their treasures.

Work

1 The following are all important dates from Henry's marriage to his first wife:
• 1533 • 1527 • 1513 • 1501 • 1509
Write each date, in chronological order, on a separate line. Beside each date, write what happened in that year. Be careful – many things happen in one of the years!

2 Why did Henry marry Catherine of Aragon? How might this be seen as unusual by today's standards?

3 Which of the following statements do you think was most important in making Henry want a divorce from Catherine of Aragon? You might want to put them in order – from 'most important reason' down to 'least'.
• Henry was bored with Catherine.
• Henry wanted to have a son.
• Henry loved Anne Boleyn.
• Henry disagreed with the Pope over religion.
Give reasons for your answer.

4 a Why did Henry want a son?
   b What do you think about his reason?

5 Why did Henry close down the monasteries? Give more than one reason.

6 Write a sentence or two to explain the following words:
   • Reformation   • Dissolution

1.4 Who'd want to marry Henry VIII?

Henry VIII had more wives than any other British king. Being his wife must have been a very tricky business. They may have enjoyed a luxurious lifestyle, but there were enormous risks involved. So which wife did he accuse of being a witch? Who did he divorce for being too ugly? And who did he have executed for having a boyfriend before she met him?

Mission Objectives

- Explain why Henry married so many women.
- Examine what happened to each of his wives.
- Advise his sixth wife on how to survive being married to Henry.

Your task is to look through the tangled love life of Henry. Imagine that you are a friend of Katherine Parr. She is a sensible, intelligent and kind 31-year-old widow and 52-year-old King Henry wants to marry her. She would be Henry's sixth wife. Despite her family's pleasure that the king has chosen her, she is a little bit worried, perhaps frightened. The marriage date has been set for 12 July 1543. Your job, as her friend, is to give her advice. Carefully read about each of Henry's previous wives and what went wrong for them. How might Katherine be able to keep the king happy? What shouldn't she do?

Let's start by looking at the ageing king…

- 52 years old.
- Cruel, bad tempered and paranoid. Once he was so convinced that someone would try to kill him as he slept that he instructed a bricklayer to brick him into his bedroom at night!
- So fat that he had to be put onto his horse with a hoist.
- He complained about headaches, fever, smallpox and malaria. His legs were covered with ulcers, which later turned to **gangrene**. One visitor wrote that Henry 'had the worst legs in the world'.

Now read about his five former wives.

Catherine of Aragon: Wife Number 1: 1509–1533

- She was Catholic.
- A Spanish princess, once married to Henry's older brother, she brought friendship with Spain.
- She was clever and popular.
- All her male babies died, which angered Henry, who wanted a male heir; she had a daughter called Mary who survived.
- Henry thought Catherine was old and boring when she reached her forties. He divorced her.

FACT!

Henry had a party to celebrate Catherine's death in 1536 (there were rumours at the time that she'd been poisoned). He even wore yellow clothes, the traditional colour of celebration!

Anne Boleyn: Wife Number 2: 1533–1536

- She was Protestant.
- She was young, attractive and very fashionable.
- She made Henry wait until it was clear they were going to marry before **consummating** their relationship.
- She had a daughter, Elizabeth. Henry sulked for weeks because he wanted a boy.
- **Miscarried** a baby boy in 1536.
- Henry accused Anne of being unfaithful with five other men. Despite having no proof, Henry had her beheaded in 1536.

FACT!

Anne was born with an extra finger on one hand. People said that this was a sign that she was a witch. Anne made enemies easily.

Jane Seymour:
Wife Number 3: 1536–1537

- She was Protestant.
- She was calm, gentle and caring. She tried hard to be friends with Henry's daughters.
- She would not consummate their relationship until they were married.
- She had a son, Edward. Henry was delighted – a boy at last!
- Jane died of an infection a few days after the birth.

FACT!

When Henry died, he was buried with Jane in Saint George's Chapel in Windsor Castle.

Catherine Howard:
Wife Number 5:
1540–1542

- She was Catholic.
- She was young, lively and very pretty.
- She flirted with lots of men… and Henry found out. She once finished off a letter to her lover with the words, 'Yours as long as life endures'. Henry was furious.
- Henry also found out that she had several serious boyfriends before she met him. A queen should not have a past like this!
- She was executed.

FACT!

When Catherine Howard found out she was going to be beheaded, she ran shouting and screaming towards Henry to beg his forgiveness. He locked the door and ignored her. Her crying ghost is still said to haunt the same corridor at Hampton Court Palace.

What happened to Katherine Parr? Find out about her life with Henry… and after.

Hungry for More?

Wise Up Words

consummate   gangrene   miscarry

Anne of Cleves:
Wife Number 4: 1540

- She was Protestant.
- Cleves was an area of what is now Germany, close to Flanders and France. Henry married Anne because it brought friendship between England and this powerful European region.
- She was serious and unfashionable. Friends tried to teach her some of Henry's favourite card games but she didn't understand them.
- Henry had seen a painting of her and liked what he saw. However, when he saw her in person, he described her as a fat 'Flanders mare [horse]'.
- Henry divorced her.

FACT!

Henry's six-month marriage to Anne was never consummated. After the divorce, Anne was given land, money and the rather strange official title of the 'King's sister'.

Work

 The Big Write!

Now write Katherine Parr a letter, giving her advice about her forthcoming marriage. In your letter include:

i details of Henry's previous five marriages.
   - What attracted Henry to each of his wives?
   - What went wrong with each marriage?
   - What happened to each of his wives?
ii top tips on how to keep Henry happy and interested in her. Remember how old he is and what sort of wife he needs now.

What did Protestants protest about?

Have you been to a church or other place of worship in the last few days… or weeks… or months? Have you prayed recently, chatted to the local vicar or religious leader, or been on a journey to the nearest cathedral?

For some people today, it is very difficult to imagine the importance of the Church in everyone's lives years ago. Today, lots of people visit a church only for weddings, christenings or funerals. It was very different in Tudor times. There were no televisions, cinemas or shopping centres. There weren't too many books or organized sports matches either. Houses weren't full of carpets, comfy chairs and sofa beds. However, there was the local church – a welcoming meeting place, a place to enjoy summer fairs, have a chat with friends and, of course, worship God.

Mission Objectives

- Explain why some people criticized the Catholic Church.
- Examine how Protestants got their name and what they believed.

The importance of religion

In Tudor times, everyone believed in God. They used religion to explain things they didn't understand. Nasty illnesses or infections were seen as punishment from God. If the harvest was bad, it was because God wished it so. They also believed that heaven and hell were real places. If you led a good life on earth and prayed regularly, then you would probably go to heaven when you died. However, if you were a bad person who committed crimes and didn't attend church regularly, then you would definitely end up in hell.

Spreading the word

By 1500, there were thousands of books available to read on many topics. There were lots of books on religion and copies of the Bible were available in English rather than Latin by 1525. For the first time, ordinary men and women could read the Bible for themselves instead of having to go to church and listen to what the priest told them. Some people started to think very deeply about the Church and wonder whether everything they had ever been told was entirely correct.

Some people began to criticize the Church. They still believed in God; they just felt that there might be different ways of worshipping him. Look at the following four main criticisms of the Church at this time.

Criticism No. 1
The Church was too rich!

The Church owned about one-third of all the land in England. An ordinary peasant had to give 10 per cent of their harvest (a **tithe**) to the priest every year. Some felt that the bishops, priests and monks lived in luxury whilst the poor suffered.

Criticism No. 2
The priests didn't lead a very 'holy' life.

Some priests had a few jobs and neglected their work. Villagers once told the Bishop of Hereford:

'The priest puts his horses and sheep in the churchyard… He was away for six weeks and made no arrangements for a substitute. Sir John [the priest] spends his time in the taverns and there his tongue is loosened to the scandal of everyone. He is living with a woman, Margaret, and he cannot read nor write and so cannot look after the parishioners' souls.'

Ordinary people thought some priests were not setting a very good example to the people in the village or town.

Criticism No. 3
Ordinary people couldn't understand the church services.

Church services were held in Latin. People said they found it difficult to feel close to God if they couldn't understand what was being said in church.

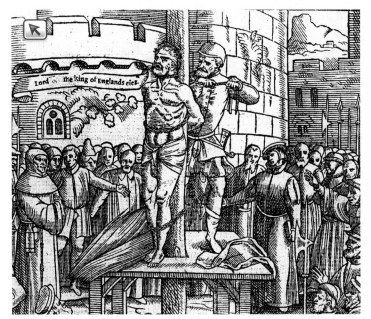

SOURCE A: *A print of the execution of William Tyndale. He was executed for translating the Bible into English so that ordinary people could read it, which was illegal at this time.*

Criticism No. 4

Poor people couldn't afford 'indulgences'.

When a person died, they went to heaven or hell. It was thought people passed through a place called **purgatory** on the way to heaven. In purgatory, people believed you were punished for any sins you may have committed whilst you were alive. It wasn't meant to be a nice place to stay for very long. So when you were alive, you could buy 'indulgences' from a bishop. This meant that you travelled through purgatory quicker. Rich people could buy lots of indulgences. Poor people didn't think it was fair. They thought that they were being punished for being poor.

In 1517, a German monk called Martin Luther wrote out a long list of criticisms of the Catholic Church and nailed it to his local church door. Remember – when we talk about religion at this time, the vast majority of people were Catholics. And this was the official religion of all European countries. So, people at the time were Christians, but they believed in worshipping God in a particular way – the Catholic way. (See the Fact! boxes.)

Luther wanted the Catholic Church to change and soon his ideas and beliefs attracted many followers. By 1529, the followers were known as **Protestants** because they protested against the Catholic Church. Now there were two religious groups in Europe who believed in a Christian version of God – the Catholics and the Protestants. However, both wanted to worship God in slightly different ways.

SOURCE B: *Martin Luther's protest against the Pope changed religion forever.*

FACT!

The **Catholic** way to worship:
- The Pope is Head of the Catholic Church and is chosen by God.
- The Bible and prayer books are written in Latin.
- A church should be a bright and colourful place to worship God, with pictures on the walls, stained-glass windows, a large stone altar, silver cups and crosses, and priests in magnificent robes.

FACT!

The **Protestant** way to worship:
- A country's monarch should be the Head of the Church.
- The Bible and prayer books should be in a language that the worshippers understand – not in Latin.
- A church should be a plain and simple place to worship God. Money shouldn't be wasted on decorations or robes for the priest.

Work

1 In your own words, explain why religion and the Church played such an important part in people's lives.

2 Explain the origin of the word 'Protestant'.

3 The year is 1517. Imagine you are Martin Luther, angry with the Catholic Church. Using the information on these pages to help you, write your own list of criticisms of the Church. You could try to make your work look old by staining it with a used teabag.

1.6 Why did the Mary Rose sink?

The *Mary Rose* was Henry VIII's favourite warship. It was completed in 1511 and is thought to be named after his younger sister Mary and the famous Tudor symbol of the rose. In July 1545, England and France were at war and the French sent a huge fleet of warships, full of French soldiers, to invade England. The English navy, including the *Mary Rose*, was sent out to fight them. Henry himself even stood and watched the action from Southsea Castle, in Portsmouth. However, when the *Mary Rose* fired her cannons at the French ships and turned to fire again… disaster struck! The ship began to sink. There was panic on board as men began to scramble to get off the sinking ship. Many of her crew couldn't swim and over 400 of them drowned.

The French invasion itself was a failure but the French soon claimed a victory of sorts. They said they had sunk the *Mary Rose*. A French admiral wrote:

'Fortune followed our fleet. The *Mary Rose*, one of their best ships, was sunk by our cannon and of the five or six hundred men which were on board, only five and thirty escaped.'

So was this true? Did the French sink the Mary Rose? If not, then why did she sink? It's time to be a History Mystery detective, so study the evidence carefully.

SOURCE A:
A painting of the Mary Rose.

Evidence B
Professor Andrew Lambert, a historian.

'To sink a ship like this with one or two hits would be astonishing.'

Evidence C
From a TV documentary broadcast in 2003 about the Mary Rose.

'When the *Mary Rose* sank in 1545, she had all the latest weapons on board… was the ship too heavy and **unstable**? Our experts have worked out that the weight of the new guns had made the ship unstable… but the weight alone was not enough to sink her.'

Evidence A
Alexzandra Hildred, a marine expert, talking after analysing the ship. In 1982, the ship was brought back up to the surface and preserved in a museum. Sadly though, half the ship had rotted.

'There are no gaping holes in the ship where a French shot might have hit… but we've only got half a ship, so we can't say any damage happened in any other place. We don't know what damage might have been done.'

Evidence D
Part of a letter written by Sir Peter Carew, younger bother of Sir George Carew. George was on board, in charge of the ship when it sank.

'There were 700 men aboard ship. The usual crew of 415 plus 300 heavily armed soldiers were concentrated in the bow and the stern [front and back of the ship]. I saw the ship heel over as she turned and only 36 were saved.'

Evidence E

*Written by one of the men who helped to cut the new **gun-ports** in 1536.*

'The new gun-ports were cut, low down, in each side of the Mary Rose to take big guns. It was hard to make them watertight. It seemed odd to be cutting holes low in the side of the ship. I remember saying that I hoped the ship would not lean over with its gun holes left open.'

Wise Up Words

gun-port   unstable

Evidence G

From the archaeologists' report after the ship was recovered in 1982.

'The ship faced towards the harbour when she was discovered. Her position, in conjunction with the evidence from the guns recovered, suggests she sank as she was executing a turn while engaging the enemy.'

Evidence F

From a TV documentary broadcast in 2003 about the Mary Rose.

'When the archaeologists recovered the *Mary Rose*, all the main gun-ports were fitted with lids. To their surprise, the lids were bound [tied] open, indicating that they could have been open when she sank.'

Evidence H

This is one of the human skulls recovered from the ship when it was brought back up to the surface in 1982. Analysis of the skulls has shown that the majority of the sailors were not British, but from southern Europe. It has been argued that this might have meant that they couldn't have properly understood the instructions of the English-speaking captain. In fact, Sir George Carew (one of the admirals on board) apparently complained that he couldn't control the crew. Could this have been because they didn't understand his language?

Work

Well, history detective, now you have the difficult task of working out why the *Mary Rose* sank. You must search through all the evidence and work out your theory. Here are some of the main theories for you to consider.

1 The French sank her.

2 The ship was too heavy and unstable.

3 The crew were difficult to control and would not follow orders.

4 The gun-ports were left open.

Step 1 Find any evidence that the French sank the ship. Does any evidence support the French claim? Can you find any evidence that shows this theory to be unlikely? What is your opinion? Make a note of your findings.

Step 2 Find evidence that the ship was too heavy or unstable. Does any evidence support this idea? If it was heavy and unstable, why was it so? Write down what you have discovered.

Step 3 Think – could the open gun-ports have sunk the *Mary Rose*? Find evidence to support this theory. Why might they have been left open? Could the crew's behaviour have anything to do with it? Why were the gun-ports so low in the water in the first place? Make notes on the evidence you have found.

Finally, you must deliver your verdict. Why did the *Mary Rose* sink? Write a short paragraph to outline your theory. Be sure to use some of the evidence you have found to back up your ideas. Why not imagine that you are writing the report for Henry VIII?

Edward VI: the boy king

Despite six marriages, Henry VIII left only three children behind when he died on 28 January 1547. Edward was nine, Elizabeth was 13 and Mary was a woman of 30. Henry had absolutely no doubt as to who he would leave in control of the country: the nine-year-old, of course! The young prince may have been the same age as a Year 5 student – but he was male! Henry believed this made him a much better choice as ruler than his older sisters. So what kind of king was young Edward? Which faith did he follow? And what did this mean for the way people worshipped God?

Mission Objectives

- Explain how and why Henry's son changed religion in England.
- Decide what kind of boy Edward VI was.

Changes in religion

As you have learned, Henry VIII had made some important changes to religion. He had closed all the monasteries (and taken their money), allowed the Bible to be read in English (not Latin) and, most importantly, made himself, and future kings and queens, Head of the Church of England (instead of the Pope). Henry didn't make any more major changes to religion and most people, including the king, still thought of themselves as Catholic.

Rood screen (to separate priest from worshippers)

Pictures to explain Bible stories

Sanctuary lamps kept permanently alight to show the continued presence of God.

Stained glass

Statue of the Virgin Mary

Expensive robes

Gold crosses, candlesticks and chalices

Stone altar

SOURCE A: *Inside a Catholic church.*

However, Henry's son Edward believed deeply in the Protestant faith. As a Protestant, he thought that the Catholic Church made people worship God in the wrong way. He felt that God should be worshipped in a plain and simple manner. As he was Head of the Church, he could alter it in any way he wished. Look at the two illustrations. **Source A** shows what a Catholic church would have looked like. **Source C** shows how it would have changed when Edward ordered people to worship as Protestants.

FACT!

Catholic priests could not marry, but Protestant priests could.

Religious turmoil

Many people, especially in the countryside, didn't like all the changes to the way they worshipped. They loved the old services and churches, and in some areas there were rebellions. The leaders of one rebellion in Cornwall saw just how ruthless young King Edward could be… he sent in his soldiers to hang the rebels from the nearest trees!

SOURCE B: *A painting of Edward VI, painted in about 1546.*

FACT!

King Edward VI could be a cruel and vicious boy. He executed his uncle for accidentally killing his favourite pet! His uncle was trying to kidnap him, though…

Wise Up Words

obituary   tuberculosis

Hungry for More?

Close to his death, Edward named his 15-year-old cousin, Lady Jane Grey, as next in line to the throne. She later became known as the 'Nine days queen'.

- Who was she?
- Why did Edward choose her?
- How did she get her nickname?
- What happened to her?

Royal coat of arms

Prayer book in English, not Latin

Wall plaques with the Lord's prayer and parts of the Bible in English

Stained glass smashed and replaced with plain glass

Plain clothes.

Pulpit for preaching the new English services

Rood screen removed

Simple wooden table

SOURCE C: *Protestant churches and ways of worshipping were much more simple.*

Poorly boy

Edward had always been a sickly child and constantly in need of a doctor's attention. He used to have his bedroom walls washed down three times a day to keep him free from disease. But by the age of 15, he was dying of a lung disease called **tuberculosis**. His hair fell out, his nails came off and his fingers and toes began to loosen and drop away at the joints. Edward died on 6 July 1553. He had no children, so, after Lady Jane Grey had ruled for only nine days, his older half-sister Mary became the new queen. She was a deeply religious Catholic. Protestant England was about to change!

Work

1 Why do you think Edward became king after his father's death and not Mary or Elizabeth?

2 a Describe what you would have seen if you had entered a Catholic church before 1547.

b Now imagine you visited the same church after Edward had made his Protestant changes and describe what you see.

3   Design and write an obituary for King Edward VI. An **obituary** briefly tells of some of the most important events, achievements and the personality of the person who recently died. Begin with Edward's birth on 12 October 1537 and end with his death on 6 July 1553 at the age of just 15.

How bloody was Bloody Mary?

Nicknames are sometimes used between friends who know each other very well. Other times, they are used by people to be nasty. Queen Mary had a very nasty nickname: Bloody Mary. But why? What could she have done to be remembered in such a horrible way? And did she deserve it?

Mission Objectives

- Examine how and why Bloody Mary got her nickname.
- Decide whether she deserved her nasty nickname.

A new queen

Mary was Henry VIII's eldest child. When she became queen in 1553, Mary was unmarried, 37 years old and a strict Catholic. Some people were delighted to have Mary as queen. They didn't like all the religious changes that had taken place in Edward's reign. They looked forward to a time when Mary would bring back the old Catholic ways.

Soon after becoming queen Mary married the Catholic King Philip of Spain. But this was seen as a bad move. Philip and the Spanish were very unpopular in England and many wondered whether the Spanish king would start interfering in the running of the country.

Religious changes... again!

As soon as she was crowned, Mary started to undo all the changes her father and brother had made.

- England was officially made a Catholic country once more.

- The Pope controlled religion again.

- The churches were redecorated with stone altars, brightly painted walls, statues and gold crosses.

- Married priests were made to leave their wives (because Catholics believe priests should be unmarried).

- Church services and prayer books were in Latin once more.

Mary's changes didn't please the Protestants, who were becoming fed up of this religious see-saw. Her message to them was simple – change religion or be punished! You might now see how Mary acquired her nickname. Now look through the sources and start to build an opinion of Mary.

SOURCE A: *A painting of Queen Mary.*

'*All the people of London rejoiced and made many great fires. They set out tables and feasted.*'

▲ **SOURCE B:** *From a diary written at the time, celebrating the arrival of the new queen.*

'*I will spare the life of Lady Jane.*'

▲ **SOURCE C:** *Lady Jane Grey was named queen by the previous king, Edward VI. She didn't last long at all. Mary's troops marched into London and arrested her. Mary promised not to kill Jane but soon ordered the execution of her, her husband and other family members!*

'*About 300 people were burned to death all over the country because they refused to worship the Catholic way. Most of these were humble shopkeepers, carpenters, farmers and housewives.*'

▲ **SOURCE D:** *From* History Alive 1 1485–1714, *by Peter Moss, 1980.*

SOURCE E: *The burning of Latimer and Ridley, two Protestants who refused to become Catholics. A person who is prepared to die for what they believe is called a* **martyr**.

'There were burnt 5 bishops, 21 ministers, 8 gentlemen, 84 workers, 100 farmers, servants and labourers, 26 wives, 20 widows, 9 girls, 2 boys and 2 infants.'

▲ **SOURCE F:** *From an essay on the history of Norfolk.*

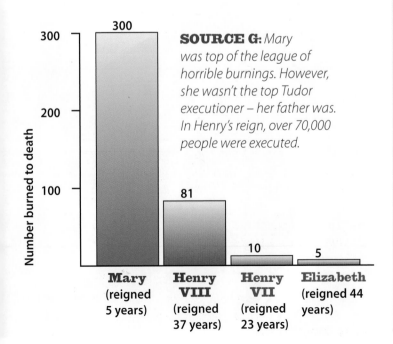

SOURCE G: *Mary was top of the league of horrible burnings. However, she wasn't the top Tudor executioner – her father was. In Henry's reign, over 70,000 people were executed.*

Wise Up Words

martyr

'… when Mary died, all the churches of London did ring, and at night did make bonfires and set tables in the street and did eat and drink and be merry…'

▲ **SOURCE H:** *From a diary written at the time of Mary's death.*

'Mary was a deeply religious woman and devoted to the same Catholic faith as her mother. All of the monarchs that have followed her have been Protestants, so Mary's history has been written by Protestant historians. They have not been kind to her.'

▲ **SOURCE I:** *An extract from a modern history book.*

Work

1 a Divide your page into two columns: 'Bloody Mary' and 'Unlucky Mary'. Read through **Sources B–I** and decide if you think they suggest whether Mary deserved her nickname or not. If you think a source does, write a brief description of it in the 'Bloody Mary' column. If you think a source doesn't, write a brief description of it in the 'Unlucky Mary' column.

   b Overall, do you think Mary deserves her nasty nickname? Give reasons for your answer.

2 **Sources B** and **H** were written by the same person. How had public opinion changed during Mary's time as queen?

3 Read **Source F**.

   a Why might you not be able to trust everything that is written in Foxe's book?

   b Do you think this book was published during Mary's reign? Give reasons for your answer.

The nastiest nursery rhyme in the world!

You've all heard it. Most of you will have sung it. Mothers sing it to babies; children sing it in nursery classes and in the playground. It sounds like a nice, friendly rhyme about a girl called Mary. But would you sing it if you really knew what each line was about? The poem is definitely about someone called Mary… but she's not a little girl! The Mary in the rhyme is rumoured to be Bloody Mary, queen from 1553 to 1558 and famous for ordering the burning of over 300 people. So what could the rhyme be about? What do all those strange words mean? And who would have written such a thing?

Mission Objectives

- Examine the hidden meaning of the popular nursery rhyme 'Mary, Mary, quite contrary'.
- Decide what religion the writer of the rhyme would have belonged to.

Read through the poem below carefully and then look through the fact boxes on these pages. Try to match them with each line. Prepare to be astonished! After you have read these pages you might think twice about singing the rhyme again.

> Mary, Mary, quite contrary,
> How does your garden grow?
> With silver bells
> And cockleshells,
> And pretty maids all in a row.

FACT!

Mary enjoyed listening to the sound of church bells. This music was unfashionable at the time.

FACT!

Mary longed for a baby. She was delighted when she thought she was pregnant soon after marrying her husband, King Philip of Spain. However, she soon found out that she wasn't pregnant at all; her stomach pains were in fact the symptoms of a terrible disease, possibly cancer. One line of the rhyme **ridicules** the fact that nothing will grow inside her.

FACT!

Mary was rumoured to have had some children, but each little girl was **stillborn**. Mary was supposed to have had them buried secretly in a long row of graves.

SOURCE A: *A portrait of Mary with her husband, Philip.*

Mary's husband wasn't very loving. King Philip hardly ever saw her during their marriage. Also, he had affairs with lots of other women. At the time, if your husband or wife was seeing other people behind your back you might be known as a **cuckold**. Which line do you think this is referring to?

Be a Top Historian

Top historians often have **different views** about significant people in history. It's perfectly OK to have a different opinion from someone else as long as you can explain your views. Why do you think a Catholic and a Protestant might have different opinions of Queen Mary?

cuckold   ridicule   stillborn

Nasty, isn't it?

Have you worked it out? Can you match the five fact boxes to the five lines of the poem? Can you see how cruel the rhyme is? It must have been made up by someone who really hated Mary. What you may have thought was a harmless nursery rhyme about a girl called Mary is really a hateful, spiteful rhyme about an awkward woman with an unfaithful husband, an unpopular taste in music and stillborn children!

FACT!

'Contrary' means 'opposite'. If a person is contrary, it often means that they take a different view just for the sake of it. Mary was accused of being awkward because she wanted to change England back to a Catholic country so soon after it had become a Protestant one.

This isn't the only cruel or nasty nursery rhyme. 'Jack and Jill' doesn't have a very happy ending, 'Rock a bye baby' ends in disaster and as for poor old 'Humpty Dumpty'… And we sing all of these to little babies. Try to find out more about some famous nursery rhymes. 'Ring a ring o' roses', 'Humpty Dumpty' and 'Little Jack Horner' all have fascinating stories surrounding them.

Hungry for More?

Work

1 a Copy out each line of the nursery rhyme but leave some space underneath it.
   b Underneath each line, explain what it really means, in your own words.

2 Do you think the writer of the rhyme was a Protestant or a Catholic? Explain your answer.

3 This rhyme was once described as a 'lot of old, nasty gossip'. What do you think this means? Explain your answer carefully.

4 Imagine you are the person who wrote the poem. Try to justify why you wrote such a spiteful poem. Use what you have learned about Mary to help you.

Elizabeth's middle way

On 17 November 1558, Mary I died. Her marriage to Philip II of Spain had produced no children, so her half-sister Elizabeth became the new queen. Elizabeth had spent much of her life as third in line to the throne and was lucky to have survived Mary's reign – Elizabeth's mother (Anne Boleyn) had taken the place of Mary's mother (Catherine of Aragon) as Henry's wife, after all! When Elizabeth heard of her half-sister's death, it is reported that she fell to her knees and said, 'This is the Lord's doing and it is marvellous in our eyes.' So which faith did Elizabeth follow? What changes did she make? And what did her arrival on the throne mean for the way people worshipped God in England?

Mission Objectives

- Analyse how Elizabeth tried to end religious turmoil in Tudor England.
- Recall which faith Elizabeth belonged to.
- Explain how this caused another Catholic clampdown.

The religious settlement

Elizabeth was going to return the country to the Protestant faith but had no intention of repeating the chaos caused by her half-brother and half-sister.

Elizabeth was not a religious fanatic and wanted to avoid the extremes of both Protestants and Catholics. That way, she hoped she would please most people and keep the country a peaceful place! Her ideas were known as her **Religious Settlement**.

A compromise with the Catholics

I'm the guv'nor!

Elizabeth made herself Governor, not Head, of the Church of England in order to please the Catholics. This meant that Catholics – if they wanted to – could still think of the Pope as Head of the Church.

Bishops were kept to please Catholics but services were in English to please Protestants.

Our Father...

Priests were allowed to marry to please the Protestants and a revised prayer book replaced the one from Edward's reign that was so hated by Catholics.

The Catholic service was changed to please the Protestants but strict Catholics, who didn't want to attend the new services, weren't severely punished. However, they had to pay a fine for staying at home and became known as **recusants**.

Did the 'middle way' work?

Although it pleased most people, **extremists** on both sides were left deeply unhappy by Elizabeth's ideas. Very strict Protestants, known as Puritans, didn't want to compromise with Catholics. They wanted to destroy the Pope and his whole religion. Strict Catholics believed that the Protestants were doing the work of the Devil and were damning the whole country to hell. In fact, the Pope claimed that Elizabeth was the daughter of a 'sorceress' and excommunicated her! He also called her a 'servant of crime' and ordered the people of England not to obey her! This made it very difficult for Elizabeth to tolerate Catholics, as any one of them could be plotting her death! As a result, she decided to make life a little tougher for the Catholics.

The Catholic clampdown

Elizabeth's chief spy, Sir Francis Walsingham, kept a close eye on all the important Catholics using informers and secret agents. New laws were passed which meant that Catholic priests would now be tried and executed for treason. The fine that recusants had to pay was heavily increased in order to force them to leave the country, but many were thrown in prison when they ran out of money. However, the prospect of being executed was not enough to stop many Catholic priests and they continued to hold their Catholic services in secret. Some were kept hidden in special hiding places called 'priest holes' to avoid detection. But Elizabeth's long reign of 44 years meant that there was to be no Catholic comeback and the Protestant faith was firmly established. Indeed, this nation remains officially a Protestant country to this day.

SOURCE A: *This secret priest hole is in Harvington Hall, Kidderminster.*

Wise Up Words

extremist   recusant   Religious Settlement

FACT!

The penalty for sheltering a Catholic priest was death but many Catholics saw it as their religious duty to keep their way of worship alive. Some priests hid up chimneys, but Walsingham's men started lighting fires every time they searched a house. The soldiers would often stop in suspected houses for days, listening for the slightest noise that would betray a hidden priest.

Be a Top Historian

Your History studies will be full of new, intriguing, difficult (and often exciting) **words and phrases**, such as 'recusant', 'excommunicate' and 'regicide'. Top historians must try to learn these words and use them correctly when talking or writing. Why not keep a 'Key Words book' or a 'Glossary of Important Words' so you have them all together?

Work

1 Explain what the word 'compromise' means.

2 Copy the following sentences into your books.
   - Elizabeth made herself Governor of the Church of England.
   - Bishops were allowed to stay in their jobs.
   - Priests were allowed to get married.
   - Edward VI's prayer book was replaced.
   - Recusants were allowed to miss church services.

   After each sentence, write 'Catholic' if it was meant to keep Catholics happy, or 'Protestant' if it was designed to please Protestants.

3 a What do you think is meant by the term 'middle way'?
   b Did Elizabeth's middle way work? Write a paragraph explaining your answer (you might want to mention the Pope!).

4 Look at **Source A**.
   a What was a priest hole?
   b Why were they needed?

Assessing Your Learning 1

Judging the Tudors

History is one of the school subjects that asks students about their opinions, and that is what's going to happen now. You need to judge who you think was the 'best' Tudor monarch from a list of four contenders – Henry VIII, Edward VI, Mary I, or Elizabeth I. And you have to give reasons for your opinion (or 'justify' it)! However, you must base your choice on a number of specific factors (or criteria), rather than just who you like best or who you think was most famous! You will be asked to rank the Tudor monarchs with these criteria in mind. Best of luck!

The Tudors are probably the best-known royal family in the world. The first Tudor, Henry VII, ruled from 1485 until his death in 1509. He made the country stronger, richer and safer than it had been for a long time. But how did the rest of the Tudor monarchs do? Your task is to work out who you think was the most successful Tudor monarch after Henry VII's death and write an extended answer. Was it his son, Henry VIII… or one of his grandchildren, Edward VI, Mary I or Elizabeth I?

Task 1

You must remember that being a Tudor king or queen wasn't all about fancy clothes, wonderful food and expensive palaces. They had a job to do as well! Below is a selection of different duties and responsibilities that a good Tudor monarch would be expected to fulfil. Firstly, explain why it would be important for a successful Tudor king or queen to do each of these five things:

> **TOP TIP:** If you are going to judge people (such as who is the best or most successful), it's important to compare them against the same criteria. So we will judge the Tudor monarchs against the same five judging criteria.

- Keep order in the country
- Remain popular
- Get land and money
- Deal with religious issues
- Leave a strong heir to become the next king or queen

Task 2

Now it's time to gather information about each of the Tudors who ruled after Henry VII. The fact boxes on the following pages will help you. You might want to make some notes.

> **TOP TIP:** As you make your notes, make sure you think about the things a good Tudor monarch would be expected to do.

FACT!

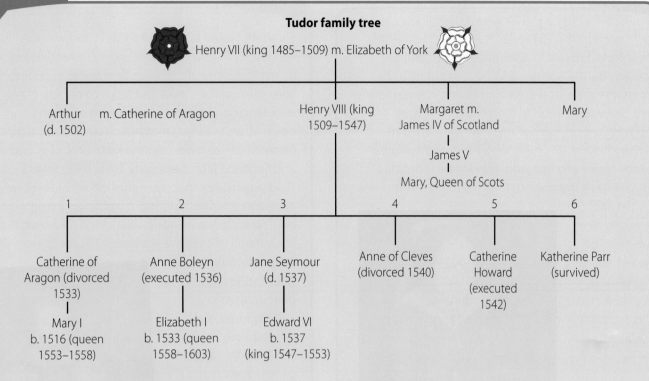

Tudor family tree

Henry VII (king 1485–1509) m. Elizabeth of York

Arthur (d. 1502)   m. Catherine of Aragon

Henry VIII (king 1509–1547)

Margaret m. James IV of Scotland

Mary

James V

Mary, Queen of Scots

1	2	3	4	5	6
Catherine of Aragon (divorced 1533)	Anne Boleyn (executed 1536)	Jane Seymour (d. 1537)	Anne of Cleves (divorced 1540)	Catherine Howard (executed 1542)	Katherine Parr (survived)
Mary I b. 1516 (queen 1553–1558)	Elizabeth I b. 1533 (queen 1558–1603)	Edward VI b. 1537 (king 1547–1553)			

FACT!

Henry VIII ruled from 1509 to 1547. As a young man, Henry was a keen sportsman and musician, and a good soldier. In old age, he was fat and bad-tempered. He inherited lots of money from his father, Henry VII, but spent it on clothes, entertainment, palaces… and war. He fought against France and Scotland, and had to raise taxes to pay for it, which made him unpopular. He didn't gain much land abroad. In 1534, he made himself Head of the Church of England and then closed down all the Catholic monasteries and took their land. When people rebelled against this, Henry rounded up 200 of the rebel leaders and executed them.

FACT!

Edward VI ruled from 1547 to 1553. Son of Henry VIII, Edward was nine years old when his father died and he became king. His uncle, the Duke of Somerset, ruled the country for him and both he and Edward were strict Protestants. They wanted churches to be simple places so they ordered church walls to be painted white and statues and stained glass to be removed. A new Prayer Book was introduced, written in English. The changes were popular with Protestants but hated by Catholics. There were rebellions against Somerset and he was eventually replaced. During Edward's reign, England was still involved in costly wars. Edward never married and died of tuberculosis, aged 15.

Mary I ruled from 1553 to 1558 and was the Catholic half-sister of Edward VI. She made England into a Catholic country again… and burned about 300 Protestants at the stake, earning the nickname Bloody Mary. She was married to King Philip II of Spain, who was very unpopular in England and tried to tell Mary how to run the country. England fought France (again) and lost land. There were rebellions against Mary's marriage to Philip, but the revolts were crushed and the rebels were executed. The couple had no children and Mary died in 1558, probably of cancer.

Elizabeth I ruled from 1558 to 1603 and was the half-sister of Mary I. Elizabeth was a Protestant but at first she allowed Catholics to worship in secret! She was popular, clever and enjoyed parties, plays and dancing. However, she never married and had no children, meaning that her distant cousin, King James VI of Scotland, became King James I of England and Scotland after her death. There were several plots against her that were crushed, including one in Ireland. In 1588, King Philip II of Spain (remember him?) planned to invade England and take over, but his Armada of ships was defeated. Elizabeth's reign is seen by many as a golden age of great poets, playwrights and explorers, such as Shakespeare, Drake and Raleigh. Land was gained abroad and new laws were passed to help the poor, which stayed in force for hundreds of years.

Task 3

Now it's time to record what you've found out about Henry, Edward, Mary and Elizabeth. For each of the four monarchs, create and complete a chart like the one below. Give each monarch a star rating (out of five) for each of their duties and responsibilities.

Which Tudor? _____		How long did they rule? _____	
Duties and responsibilities	**What they did well**	**What they did badly**	**Star rating** ★ = poor ★★★★★ = brilliant
Keep order in the country			
Remain popular			
Get land and money			
Deal with religious issues			
Leave a strong heir to become the next king or queen			
		Total stars	

Task 4

Now it's time to make a judgement! Who was the most successful Tudor monarch? Was it Henry VIII, Edward VI, Mary I or Elizabeth I? You must write an extended answer to this question making sure you:

- write about each of the monarchs featured in this assessment

- say what each monarch did well… and what they did badly

- explain your criteria for judging them

- conclude your answer with who you think was the most successful… and why. You might mention your star rating here too. Why have you awarded the stars you have given to each one?

Assessing your work

Look at the success criteria for this task to help you plan and evaluate your work.

Good	In a **good** extended answer, you would…	• describe each monarch • say what each monarch achieved (or didn't achieve) • use dates and historical terms correctly • have a basic structure.
Better	In a **better** extended answer, you would…	• describe each monarch in detail • select and use information to explain what each monarch did successfully (or not so successfully) • use the correct dates and proper historical terms • produce well-structured work and include a conclusion about which monarch you think was the most successful.
Best	In the **best** extended answer, you would…	• explain how you decided to judge the monarchs • show why you think some Tudor monarchs were more successful than others • select, organize and use relevant information and use the correct historical terms to produce structured work • include a conclusion that sums up your findings.

Hungry for More?

Where does the first Tudor monarch (Henry VII) fit in? Find out about Henry VIII's father (and Mary, Elizabeth and Edward's grandfather) and work out where he'd fit in on your Tudor line up. Judge him on the same criteria that you've judged the other four. Would he be the most successful… or not?

FACT!

To help you get started with the Hungry for More? task, you might like to research who Henry VII married and why…

The man who wanted to know everything

During the Middle Ages, all books had to be written out by hand. This took a long time, so books were both rare and expensive. The work was done by monks and most books were bibles, prayer books or religious stories. But all that started to change in 1451 when the printing press was invented (see **Source A**). This special machine, which printed pages, meant that books could be produced far quicker and much more cheaply. And as more books were published, more people wanted to read them. Soon it became fashionable to write books too. There were books on fishing, hunting, chess, medicine, travel and different religions. Printing meant sailors, explorers and traders could have more copies of accurate maps too. No longer did people have to ask the local priest why something happened – they could open a book and find out for themselves!

Mission Objectives

- Explain what is meant by the word 'renaissance'.
- Examine what triggered the Renaissance.
- Explore why Leonardo da Vinci was such an important 'Renaissance man'.

SOURCE A: *A printing press, 1530. Many people have compared the invention of the printing press with the invention of the Internet. Both allowed ideas and information to spread far more quickly than they had before.*

Information explosion!

Educated people soon began to read the old books written by the Greeks and Romans who lived before Christ. They found, to their amazement, that the Greeks and Romans had known a lot more than people realized. Across Europe, writers, sculptors, doctors, mathematicians, scientists and architects started to realize that some of their current ideas were wrong and that there were often better ways of doing things. They began to ask questions and experiment with new ideas. For years, people had accepted that the Bible had all the answers to their questions. Now, educated people wanted to find things out for themselves.

Leonardo da Vinci

One man who was fascinated by these ideas was Leonardo da Vinci, who was born in Italy in 1452. He was a painter, scientist, engineer, musician and writer. He has been called 'the man who wanted to know everything'. And he was so obsessed with finding out new things that he made himself a 'to-do' list every day (see **Source B**).

A genius?

Many of Leonardo's ideas concerned war and flying. He dreamed of building some of the finest weapons the world had ever seen and of designing a machine that would allow a man to fly like a bird. He also designed helicopters, canals, cranes, a snorkel, a lifebelt and a submarine. He even made an alarm clock that tipped water onto a sleeping person to wake them up! Some of his sketches clearly show that he thought of doing things hundreds of years before anyone else.

SOURCE B: *This list is copied from Leonardo's original Italian notes.* ▼

- Make glasses to see the moon and magnify it.
- Find out how they built the tower of Ferraro.
- Analyse the movement of the tongue of a woodpecker.
- Describe the jaw of a crocodile.
- Find the Frenchman who has promised to tell me the size of the sun.
- Find out how you run on ice.

SOURCE D: *Leonardo designed a 'tank' made from wood and steel with a cannon in the 'tortoise shell' roof. The first tanks were not used in war until 1916.*

▲ **SOURCE C:** *This is a self-portrait of Leonardo in later life. He was a vegetarian, which was very unusual at the time. He used to buy caged birds at the market and then set them free!*

A world reborn?

Leonardo was not alone in his fascination with learning about the world. Over the years, many men would make fascinating discoveries in the worlds of science, medicine and engineering. This period of discovery is known as the **Renaissance**, an Italian word meaning 'rebirth'. To many, it seemed as if their new knowledge and ideas were allowing them to see the world clearly for the first time ever. They really felt that they had been reborn.

Hungry for More?

Leonardo was very secretive about some of his ideas. When describing them in his notes, he wrote backwards, from right to left, so they could only be read in a mirror. Why do you think he wanted some of his ideas kept secret?

Work

1 Copy and complete the following sentences.
   a Leonardo da Vinci was born in _____ in 1452.
   b Many people consider Leonardo to be a _____ .
   c Many of his ideas are concerned with _____ and _____ .
   d In order to keep his ideas secret, he would often write _____ .
   e Leonardo would make a _____ of new things to find out every day.

2 Why and how did the invention of the printing press help lead to greater learning in Europe?

3 Look at **Source B**. What does this list tell you about the sort of man Leonardo was?

4 Why is this period of history often referred to as the Renaissance?

5 Be like Leonardo! Design your own alarm clock that tips water on your head to wake you. (Remember, no electricity!)

As the Tudor age began, Europeans were beginning to make some amazing discoveries about their world. By this time, most educated people realized that the Earth is a **sphere**, but didn't really know its true size or how much land there was. So how did this change? Why were people so keen to find out more about the world? And who were the important individuals in this age of exploration?

Mission Objectives

- Explore what Europeans knew of the world at the beginning of the Tudor age.
- Summarize why explorers were so keen to discover new routes to foreign lands.
- Explain the significance of key explorers.

Who knows what?

By the early 1400s, Europeans obviously knew about European lands such as England, Spain, Scotland, Portugal, France and Italy. They also knew of the Holy Land (then ruled by Turks), much of Africa, Russia and lands in the east such as China and India. Other than that, they weren't really sure!

Money, money, money

One of the main reasons why Europeans were so keen to travel to foreign lands was to make lots of money. For centuries, Europeans had travelled by land to places like India and China where they bought wonderful silk cloth, spices, perfumes, jewels and porcelain (see **Source B**). When these exotic and very fashionable goods arrived back in Europe, they were sold at very high prices and the traders or merchants made huge profits.

What Happened When? | 1489

In 1489, a coin called a 'sovereign' was first created. The coin featured Henry VII on one side and the royal coat of arms on the other, and was made of 23-carat gold!

SOURCE A: *This map, drawn by Henricus Martellus around 1489, shows what Europeans thought the world looked like at that time.*

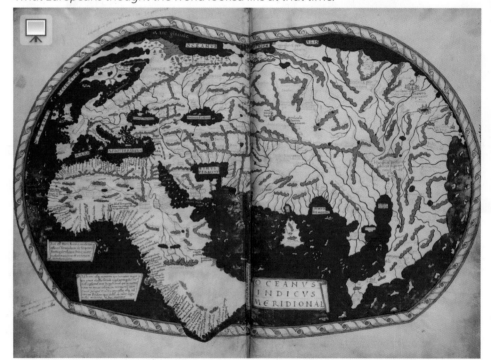

SOURCE B: *This wall hanging from the late sixteenth century shows traders in India.*

Travel problems

However, the journey by land from Europe to India and China (and back) was very dangerous and could take over three years – and the Turks charged traders a fortune to pass through their lands. As a result, some traders wanted to find an alternative route to these faraway lands… perhaps by sea?

New technology

Fortunately for the traders, a number of improvements in ship-building and **navigation** were taking place at this time. For example, better sails made ships easier to steer and an ancient Greek invention called an **astrolabe** was developed to help sailors figure out how far north or south they were whilst at sea (see **Source C**). This meant that the traders might not have to travel by land to get to China and India at all.

A new theory

By the 1490s, there was a growing belief that it was possible to reach China and India by sailing west across the Atlantic Ocean in order to reach the East. In other words, they could sail all around the Earth by sea, instead of having to go overland. Remember, people had absolutely no idea that the continents of North and South America were in the way, so some thought that this was a perfectly good idea! One man, Christopher Columbus, decided to test this theory in 1492. Some people thought he was mad. Columbus just hoped that it would make him rich!

Wise Up Words

astrolabe   native   navigation
sphere   voyage

SOURCE C: *This astrolabe was owned by Sir Francis Drake, the first British person to sail around the world.*

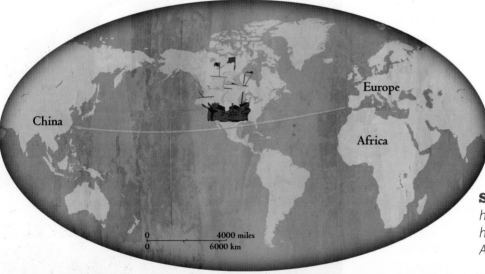

China   Europe   Africa

0   4000 miles
0   6000 km

SOURCE D: *Columbus thought he could sail to China like this. He had no idea that North and South America were in the way!*

Work

1 Explain why some Europeans were so keen to find a new route to the eastern lands of China and India.

2 Look at **Source A**.
   a How can you tell that a lot was known about the west coast of Africa in 1489, but not the east coast?
   b Make a list of some of the places in the world that we know exist today that Europeans had not discovered in 1489. You might need to look in a modern atlas.

3 a What is an astrolabe?
   b How might an astrolabe have helped Christopher Columbus?

4 In your own words, describe Columbus' plan to reach China and India.

Setting out

Columbus first tried to borrow money for his journey from the kings of Portugal, France and England. They all refused. Eventually, tempted by the promise of gold and spices, Queen Isabella of Spain funded his **voyage**.

He then bought three ships, the *Pinta*, the *Niña* and the *Santa María*, and hired around100 men to act as his crew. He set off on 3 August 1492.

All at sea

The voyage went well for about six weeks. The crew occasionally went swimming, fished and sang together. Columbus read passages from the Bible to the men. However, by early October the crew were becoming unhappy. Water and food supplies were getting low and there was no sign of India or China. Was Columbus wrong? Perhaps the world wasn't a sphere after all? Were they about to fall off the edge of the world?

Land, land!

On 12 October, Columbus' luck changed when a lookout on the *Pinta* spotted land. Columbus sailed ashore and named the island San Salvador, meaning 'Holy Saviour' (it is now also known as Watling Island). He spent the next few months sailing around the Caribbean islands and Cuba. He found **natives** of these islands and kidnapped six of them to take back to Queen Isabella! He also took some gold, several fish and some parrots.

A new hero

Columbus returned home to a hero's welcome. He made three more trips to these new islands and also landed on the South American mainland. Until his death in 1506, Columbus still thought he'd found a new route to India or China. Native Americans were even called Indians and today, some people still refer to them as American 'Indians'. We still call the islands he visited the West Indies too. Columbus had no idea that he had found the new continents of North and South America, which Europeans did not know existed. Only in later years, after explorers had found other lands, did people realize that Columbus had discovered a 'new world'.

---

10 October 1492

'He navigated west-south-west. They went ten miles an hour and at times twelve and sometimes seven... The men could now bear no more. They complained of the long voyage. But Admiral Columbus cheered them as best he could, holding out bright hopes of the gains they could make. He said God would keep them safe.'

▲ **SOURCE A:** *From the logbook of Columbus' ships.*

SOURCE B: *Columbus' voyage of discovery changed the history of world exploration.*

Columbus – the first of many

Columbus' success inspired other explorers. The promise of wealth, better maps, compasses and sails meant that more people would travel the world.

- Vasco da Gama (from Portugal) – In 1498, he proved it was possible to reach India by sailing around the bottom of Africa and up its eastern coast.
- Amerigo Vespucci (from Italy) – From 1499 to 1504, he continued exploring the area where Columbus had sailed and even further down the South American coast. Many people think America was named after him.
- Ferdinand Magellan (from Portugal) – On 20 September 1519, five ships and 270 men set off on a journey around the world. Magellan, the leader, died on the voyage but his crew sailed on. One ship and eighteen of his original crew made it home in 1522.
- John Cabot (from Italy) – In 1497, he tried to reach Asia by sailing north-west. He sailed to Canada.

FACT!

The lookout on Columbus' ship, *Pinta*, who first spotted land, was called Rodrigo. As Queen Isabella had offered a reward for the first man to see land, Rodrigo thought he was about to receive a pension every year for life. However, Columbus kept the money for himself... he argued that he had actually spotted land first but just wasn't sure, so it should be his reward.

FACT!

Explorers brought back interesting new goods from their voyages. These items had never been seen in Europe before… and were a huge success. They included tomatoes, pineapples, tobacco, potatoes, turkeys and cocoa.

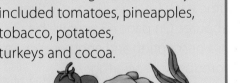

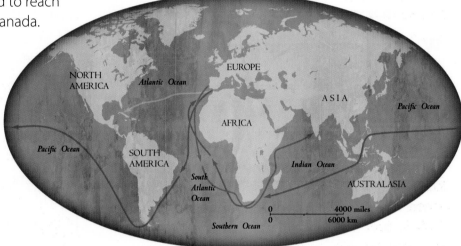

→ Columbus - first to America in 1492
→ Da Gama - first to India in 1498
→ Magellan - first trip around the world in 1522

SOURCE C: *This map shows the routes of three famous explorers' voyages.*

Work

1 Write the following sentences into your books. Next to each sentence, write whether it is true or false. If you believe a sentence is false, write the correct sentence underneath.
   - Vasco da Gama reached India by sailing around the bottom of Italy.
   - America is named after the British explorer Amerigo Vespucci.
   - Ferdinand Magellan did not survive the first full journey around the world.
   - John Cabot, from Scotland, discovered Australia.

2 Read **Source A** carefully.
   a What examples can you give to show that Columbus was a strong leader?

   b Make up your own logbook entry for 12 October. Remember to mention Rodrigo.

3 a Where did Columbus think he had discovered in 1492?
   b Was he correct?

4 Explorers were treated as heroes at this time – why do you think this was?

5 **The Big Write!**

Imagine you are a ship's captain returning with previously unknown goods from distant lands. Write a letter to a friend describing some of these new goods. (Good luck describing a turkey!)

We are all different. We all look, dress and behave differently. We don't all have the same amount of money either. It was just the same in Tudor times. You could place people into groups. Historians often use the word **class** instead of group. In 1587, a man called William Harrison published a book called *Description of England*. He wrote, 'We divide our people into four groups: **gentlemen**, **citizens**, **yeomen** and **labourers**.' But what did he mean?

Read about the four groups mentioned in Harrison's book. Later on you will be asked to match each group to a house, a description of their life and a picture.

Who were the gentlemen?

These people were very, very rich. They lived in huge country houses with lots of rooms in which to hold dinner parties, dances and music concerts. They owned lots of land and people paid them rent to farm it. Some of these men helped the king or queen to run the country. Other gentlemen were not quite so rich but still lived in large houses with plenty of land. Gentlemen (and their wives and families) made up about 5 per cent of the population.

Who were the citizens?

These people lived in towns and were still rich. Some made money from buying and selling goods, such as wool, jewellery, food, wine or cloth. These men were sometimes called **merchants**. They lived in fine town houses and had servants. They made up about 5 per cent of the population.

Who were the yeomen?

They were farmers. They either owned their land or rented land from a gentleman. They often lived in a medium-sized farmhouse and made quite a good living from farming crops (wheat or barley, for example) or cattle, pigs or sheep. They employed people to work on their farms and some yeomen even had servants. Yeomen and their families made up about 30 per cent of the population.

Who were the labourers?

These people were similar in status to the peasants of the Middle Ages. If they lived in the country – and most did – they would work on a farm. Some had their own small piece of land to grow their own vegetables and keep a few chickens. Some labourers lived in towns and might have worked as carpenters, tailors, shoemakers or bricklayers. Labourers made up about 60 per cent of the population.

Now study the following four photographs. Try to identify a home each for a gentleman, citizen, yeoman and labourer. On page 43 you will be asked to match a description and another picture to each of the groups of people too.

HOME A

HOME B

HOME C

HOME D

Wise Up Words

citizen class gentleman
labourer merchant pauper
Poor Law yeoman

What Happened When?

1947

In 1947, historic buildings started to become 'listed' after many were lost during World War Two. This means that they are carefully protected and looked after. There are many Tudor buildings on this list that still survive today.

'He eats well: bread, beer and beef, good food… full bellyfuls. He works hard: making hay, shearing corn, his workers are happy to farm for him.'

▲ DESCRIPTION A

'His house has walls of earth, a low thatched roof, few rooms… a hole in the wall to let out smoke… he is very poor and has to labour hard for his living.'

PICTURE A

PICTURE C

PICTURE B

'Every day he wears silks, velvets, satins and such like. He once gave away a pair of perfumed gloves with 24 small gold buttons, in each button a small diamond.'

▲ DESCRIPTION C

'He brought back with him wine, olive oil, currants, silk, clothes and dates. He sold them to a man who then sold them in London.'

▲ DESCRIPTION D

PICTURE D

What about the poorest of the poor?

Even lower than the poorest labourers were the **paupers** – people who had no jobs and relied on charity. Some paupers were given permission to beg and wore special badges to show this. Others went to their local church to collect 'relief' – a few pennies to buy clothes or bread. Local people were taxed to pay for this.

In 1601, a **Poor Law** put the paupers into four categories. Each group was treated differently:

1 pauper children – given work

2 sick paupers – looked after in special homes

3 fit paupers – given work (they received food and drink as payment)

4 lazy, idle paupers – whipped, then sent to a House of Correction (a place where they were forced to work, then their products were sold).

Again, people were taxed to pay for the relief provided through the Poor Law.

SOURCE A: *This illustration shows a gentleman ignoring a beggar.*

Hungry for More?

What do you think should be done about homeless people in today's world? Do some reasearch into what has recently been said in the media about this issue.

Work

1 In your own words, explain the meaning of the following:
- gentleman
- citizen
- yeoman
- labourer
- pauper

2 a Copy the chart below carefully.
  b Complete the chart by looking closely at the information on pages 40 to 42. Match the descriptions and pictures on these pages to the correct group or 'class' of people.
  c Now choose one of the sets of sources you have matched together and explain how you made your decision. For example, if you choose the sources of a gentleman you might construct your sentences like this:
- I think picture _____ shows a gentleman because…
- I think home _____ would belong to a gentleman because…
- I think description _____ is that of a gentleman because…

3 a What was a pauper?
  b How were the poor looked after in Tudor times?

Class	Which home do you think he lived in? (Choose from HOMES A to D)	Which description matches him? (Choose from DESCRIPTIONS A to D)	What does he look like? (Choose from PICTURES A to D)
Gentlemen			
Citizens			
Yeomen			
Labourers			

Have you ever had an adult tell you how tough school was in 'their day'? Bet you have! They would probably have told you about the scary teachers, how long detentions were and the horrible food. In fact, some of you sitting in a classroom today probably think your school life is really tough – so it's a good job you didn't go to school in Tudor times.

Mission Objectives

- Recall at least five facts about education in Tudor England.
- Compare today's schools with those in Tudor times.

A Tudor child's education often depended on how wealthy their father was. It wasn't free to attend school, and poor families couldn't afford the school fees. As a result, poor children would probably start work when they were five or six years old.

Richer families might send their children to a **grammar school**, so called because they taught mainly Latin and Greek grammar. Latin was the language used by businessmen and merchants throughout Europe. So any ambitious father would make sure his child was taught at one of Britain's best grammar schools.

The picture below is based on a classroom at a school near Chester called Banbury Grammar School, which opened in 1594. Nearly every large town had a grammar school in Queen Elizabeth's reign. The key on page 45 will help you understand what's going on.

FACT!

Schools closed for two weeks at Christmas and two weeks at Easter. A school week was often Monday to Saturday – and there were no summer holidays.

Hungry for More?

Using your local library, find out details of the oldest school in your area.
- How old is it?
- How has the school changed over the years?
- Are there any things that have stayed the same and provide us with evidence of the past?
- Are there any famous ex-students?

birch   grammar school   hornbook
quill pen

▶ **SOURCE B:** *Genuine school rules from England, including Manchester Grammar School and Oundle School.*

School rules

You will be beaten for:

- *arriving late*
- *not learning a passage from the Bible off by heart*
- *forgetting your books*
- *hitting another pupil*
- *playing with dice or cards*
- *going to an alehouse at lunchtime*
- *losing your school cap*
- *making fun of another pupil*
- *stealing, swearing or lying*
- *wearing a dagger or bringing a stick or a bat to school – only meat knives allowed.*

▶ **SOURCE A:** *A typical school timetable for a day. Lessons must have been dull – no computers, televisions, Internet or interactive whiteboards. And a lot of the lessons had to be learned off by heart.*

6:00am – Day starts – Registration
6:15am – Prayers
7:00am – Latin grammar
9:00am – Maths
11:00am – Lunch (bread, beef, dried fruit, ale)
12:00pm – Greek grammar
2:00pm – Essays
3:00pm – Divinity (Religious Studies)
4:00pm – Homework given out
4:45pm – Prayers/Bible reading
5:00pm – Home time

Key

1 **School Rules:** Tudor schools were very strict. You could be beaten for being late, not learning to spell properly, swearing, making fun of another student, forgetting books or gambling. Look at **Source B** and compare some of your school rules to those in Tudor times.

2 **The birch:** A bundle of **birch** twigs or even a whip were used to hit children. A punishment session would be held once a week! Some school badges actually showed boys being hit with a cane. Why do you think that this type of punishment has stopped in the last 50 years?

3 **A portrait:** A painting of the king, queen or the man who founded the school would often be displayed in the classroom. Does your school display any portraits or photographs of important people?

4 **Printed books:** Each student was expected to bring their own Bible to Banbury Grammar School. Why do you think that many of the other books were kept behind the teacher?

5 **Girls in school:** Girls were allowed to study at Banbury until they were nine or they had learned to read English. It wasn't common to see girls in a classroom and many were educated at home. Some free places were allocated to boys who were poor but clever.

6 **Children studying:** What lesson do you think is taking place here? What makes you think this? Children wrote with a **quill pen**, made from a feather, and often read out loud from a **hornbook** (it looked like a wooden bat). What else do you think it could be used for? One side would have the alphabet and the Lord's Prayer on it. The other side was left blank and was used to practise writing or maths on.

7 **Teacher:** Sometimes called a schoolmaster. Teachers were always men and could be very strict. In one school, a particularly strict teacher used to whip students every morning in winter… just to warm himself up!

8 **Toys:** Balls, spinning tops and hoops were used at break times. The students would usually have two or three breaks each day, bringing bread, beef and beer with them from home. The day would begin at 6:00am and home time could be 12 hours later. Parents had to buy candles in the winter so their children could read – and they had to buy any additional books they might need too! In fact, a year's books might cost over £10, which was about as much as a teacher earned each year!

Work

1 Write two sentences to describe each of the following:
   - birch
   - quill pen
   - hornbook
   - grammar school

2 Why did so few poor children go to school in Tudor times?

3 Make a list of five similarities and five differences between your school and a school in Tudor times.

4 Imagine you are a student at the Tudor version of your school. Using the information provided on these pages, write a paragraph describing a typical day at your school. Use **Source A** to help you. The title should be, 'A day in the life of (insert name) at (insert name) Grammar School.'

5 Look at **Source B**.
   a Which of the 'offences' on the list would you not be punished for in your school?
   b Explain why you wouldn't be punished.

How did people have fun in Tudor times?

There was no television or radio in Tudor times. People couldn't go to the cinema, play a computer game or with their mobile phones, or listen to CDs either. Instead, they had to make their own entertainment. You will easily recognize some of the games and sports… others might leave you reaching for the sick bucket! So how did the Tudors have fun?

Mission Objectives

- Examine how and why Tudor entertainment differed from the types of entertainment we enjoy today.

Go to public executions: Tudor people loved to see criminals being killed. Poorer criminals were hanged; richer ones were beheaded with a sword. In London, spectators complained when one hangman executed 20 people at once. They were not happy because they wanted the criminals to be killed one at a time so they could see the expression on each prisoner's face!

Bet on blood sports: A bear or a bull would be tied to a post and attacked by a pack of wild dogs. Sometimes two cocks or chickens would be forced to attack each other after having their beaks sharpened and metal blades attached to their legs. People would bet on the results. Some successful bears, such as Harry Hunks, Tom of Lincoln and Blind Robin, became as famous as some footballers and pop stars are today. (See **Source A**).

Play Cudgels or Shin-hacking: Two simple games for two players.

To play **Cudgels** – two people stand opposite each other, each holding a heavy stick. They take it in turns to hit each other. The person left standing wins.

To play **Shin-hacking** – two people stand opposite each other in their biggest, heaviest boots. They take it in turns to kick each other as hard as they can. The person left standing wins.

> '*A large bear on a long rope was tied to a stake. The many great English bulldogs were brought in and first shown to the bear, which afterwards they baited one after another. The excellence and guts of such bulldogs were shown, for although they were much struck and mauled by the bear, they did not give in, but had to be pulled off by sheer force and their mouths kept open with long sticks with a broad iron–piece fixed to the top.*'

▲ **SOURCE A:** *A 1599 diary entry describes bear-baiting.*

Watch the strolling players: Groups of actors travelled from village to village and acted out well-known stories or plays. They also carried news and gossip. Often, they were joined by acrobats, jugglers, musicians and puppeteers. Plays soon became so popular that special theatres were built.

Join in a football match: One village or town would take on another. The ball (a pig's bladder full of sawdust and peas) would be carried, kicked and thrown across the land between the two villages. The winning 'team' was the one that got the ball into the centre of the other village. In 1602, a spectator wrote, 'The players go home as if they have been at war – bleeding heads, bones broken and out of joint, and such bruises as serve to shorten their days.'

All the fun of the fair: There were no roller-coaster rides or arcade games. Instead, a fair was a large noisy market full of goods to buy, food to eat and entertainment to watch (or join in with). Fire-eaters, tightrope walkers, sword-fighting and dog racing were all popular, as were most of the other sports and entertainment on these pages.

SOURCE B: *The 'Cotswold Olimpick Games' started in 1612 and were held every year during* **Whitsun**. *Can you see men sword-fighting, playing Shin-hacking and throwing javelins?*

Work

1 a Which forms of Tudor entertainment seem unpleasant or cruel to us today or have since been made illegal?

   b Why do you think some of the sports and entertainments have been banned?

2 a Why would a band of strolling players coming to town be such a big event in Tudor times?

   b In what ways is the modern game of football different from that played in Tudor times?

Fun-loving nation

Ordinary people had tough lives and worked long hours in Tudor times. So, when they had any spare time, they would set out in search of serious fun! Drinking, singing, playing games and dancing were as popular back then as they are now… and a foreign visitor in the 1600s wrote that 'no nation beats them in their variety of sports and entertainment'.

Hungry for More?

Some towns became famous for their huge fairs held every year. London held a cloth fair, Nottingham held a goose fair and Birmingham held a gingerbread fair, for example. Why not try to find out about one of these? Or find out about a similar fair elsewhere. The goose fair is still going strong today.

'It does seem strange that the Tudor people who so much admired beauty in music, poetry, drama and architecture should have taken such delight in cruel, blood-thirsty "sports" which involved the torture of animals.'

◀ **SOURCE C:** A modern historian writes about the Tudor people's love of such 'sports' as bear-baiting and cockfighting.

'There were a great many inns, taverns and beer gardens scattered about the city, where much amusement may be had in eating, drinking, fiddling and the rest.'

▲ **SOURCE D:** A Swiss tourist describes Tudor London. Having a beer at a local 'pub' was just as popular in Tudor England as it is today.

SOURCE E: People enjoying themselves in Tudor times.

Kings and queens enjoyed sport too. Henry VIII enjoyed tennis, archery, skittles and wrestling. In 1520, he challenged King Francis of France to a wrestling match. The two men actually wrestled each other but Henry fell over and lost after a few minutes. He was so humiliated that he claimed he had been tripped up! Mary, Queen of Scots, had her own billiards table and also enjoyed the odd game of golf – so did Charles I, who played in a field near Newcastle a few months before he had his head chopped off.

Most games, sports and festivals would take place on holy days and other festivals such as Christmas, May Day and Midsummer Eve. People would attend church services in the morning and have fun later on in the day. The word 'holiday' comes from 'holy day'.

FIVE MEN'S MORRIS
A BOARD GAME FOR TWO PLAYERS

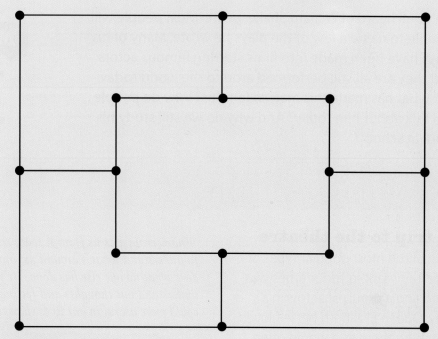

Instructions:
1 Draw the board pictured above on a large piece of card.
2 Both players have five counters or coins.
3 Each player takes it in turn to place a counter on a dot.
4 The aim is to get three counters in a row or sequence.
5 Each player tries to block the other from making a run of three.
6 If, when all the ten counters are on the board, neither player has won, the counters can be moved, one step at a time. A player can only slide to an open dot, one move at a time.
7 The first to get three in a row is the winner.

SOURCE F: *In Tudor times, drinking, singing and dancing were always popular. Dice, cards, draughts, chess and dominoes were popular too – so was a basic board game called Merelles or Five Men's Morris.*

Work

1 Look at **Source E**. People would have enjoyed themselves like this in Tudor times. With a partner, list as many games and activities as you can see. You should be able to spot at least eight, including the boy tied up in a knot!

2 **The Big Write!**

Write a conversation between two Tudor people. One has never been into the local town to see a fair or festival, and doesn't know whether to go or not. The other has been to them a lot and is keen for their friend to go too. You could set this out as a play script, with the names in the margin, and no speech marks.

3 Where does the word 'holiday' come from?

4 Design a poster advertising a local fair in Tudor times. Remember to include key facts such as the day of the fair (it must be on the day of a religious festival) and details of the entertainment taking place.

Be a Top Historian

It's important to know that studying history should not just be about kings and queens, battles, wars and politics. To truly understand the history of a country, it's just as important to discover how **ordinary people** lived their lives!

We've all heard of William Shakespeare. Most people will be able to name a few of the plays he wrote. Many of his plays have been made into films starring famous actors and they are all still performed around the world today. But what has made this man so famous? Why do people still talk about him today? And why do we still study his work at school?

Mission Objectives

- Explore how the theatre became popular in Tudor times.
- Explain why William Shakespeare became the most famous Englishman in the world.

A trip to the theatre

One of the most popular types of entertainment in Tudor times was watching a group of actors in a play. Queen Elizabeth herself loved watching them and would often get a group of actors to visit her palace to act for her. In 1576, an actor named James Burbage saw a chance to make some money from this and built the first successful permanent theatre, which was located in Shoreditch, just north-east of London. Burbage made a fortune and soon other theatres were built nearby, such as the Fortune, the Globe and the Swan (see **Source A**). By 1600, watching a play was probably one of the most popular forms of entertainment in the country.

'Engineering gets us from A to B; science helps us to understand what's around us; but Shakespeare does what no one else has done. He makes us understand our thoughts and feelings and what could more useful in our lives than that?'

SOURCE A: *Fiona Shaw, a television presenter on BBC'S Greatest Britons series, 2002*

Theatres were round with no roof, so plays were usually performed during the day.

There were different prices for the seats in the **galleries**, depending on how close you were or whether your seat had a cushion or not (1–3 pence).

Flying a flag, blowing a trumpet or firing a cannon announced the start of a play.

The stage jutted out into the pit.

There were no female actors; all parts were played by men or boys.

Money was collected and stored in locked boxes. This is where we get the term 'box office'.

Pies, beer, fruit and soup could be bought during the performance.

The **pit** was the area near the stage where people could stand and watch for only a small price (½ penny).

SOURCE B: *This picture shows the inside of the Swan Theatre, which was built in the 1590s.*

Superstar playwrights

The popularity of the theatre led to people earning a living by writing new plays. Many of these **playwrights** are still well known today, such as Christopher Marlowe and Ben Jonson. But by far the most famous is William Shakespeare.

Shakespeare is thought to have started writing plays in 1588. He wrote at least 37 and even acted in some of them. His plays are famous all over the world. They are important because they not only show us how people lived and thought in Tudor times, but also because Shakespeare wrote about everyday human emotions, such as love, hate and jealousy. We all experience these feelings today and people can relate to them whatever century his plays are set in. **Source D** highlights some of the themes in Shakespeare's plays.

SOURCE C: *William Shakespeare.*

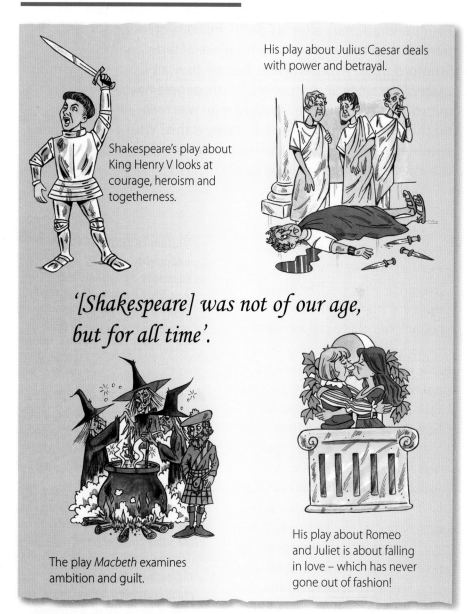

His play about Julius Caesar deals with power and betrayal.

Shakespeare's play about King Henry V looks at courage, heroism and togetherness.

'[Shakespeare] was not of our age, but for all time'.

The play *Macbeth* examines ambition and guilt.

His play about Romeo and Juliet is about falling in love – which has never gone out of fashion!

SOURCE D: *Ben Jonson, another famous writer at the time, wrote the quotation in the centre of these cartoons. What do you think he meant?*

Work

1 a What was James Burbage's claim to fame?
   b Why do you think theatre is less popular today than it was in Tudor times?

2 a Describe the sights, sounds and smells that a visitor to a theatre would have experienced in Shakespeare's time.
   b How did Tudor theatre visits compare to visiting the theatre today?

3 Design a poster advertising one of Shakespeare's plays in London in the 1590s. Remember to include the venue, date and time of the production, the entry cost, the name of the play and perhaps even a few lines to encourage people to attend.

4 a What Shakespeare plays have you seen or read?
   b Why do you think he is popular throughout the world and is still studied in schools today?

Shakespeare or Fakespeare?

William Shakespeare is the most famous author in British history. Four hundred years after his death, millions of tourists travel from all over the world to visit his place of birth and his grave in Stratford-upon-Avon, England. But are they all visiting the wrong place? Ever since Shakespeare's death, people have repeatedly questioned whether the Stratford man was really responsible for the works of Shakespeare. But why is this? Who do they think wrote them instead? And has the whole world been fooled by the most amazing hoax in history?

Mission Objectives

- Investigate the debate into who actually wrote Shakespeare's plays and poems.
- Decide whether you are a Stratfordian or an anti-Stratfordian.

Nobody denies that there was a man called William Shakespeare who was born in Stratford-upon-Avon in 1564. There is no argument that he got married aged 18, had three children and moved to London to become an actor. He is listed among actors who performed twice for Queen Elizabeth and his name appears as one of the owners of the Globe theatre. But what people argue about is whether this man was responsible for writing plays such as *Romeo and Juliet* and *Macbeth*. Those who believe he wrote the plays are known as **Stratfordians**, and those who doubt that he did are called **anti-Stratfordians**. Look at the following sources and decide which side you're on!

'Unlike other writers of the period, not a single manuscript [original copy of a play] or letter exists in Shakespeare's own handwriting. Nothing survives of a literary nature that connects William of Stratford, the man, with any of the 'Shakespeare' works.'

▲ **SOURCE A:** Matthew Cossolotto, former President of the Shakespeare Oxford Society.

'Italian culture and literature were widespread in all of Elizabethan literature and drama – not just Shakespeare. There were many sources for any intelligent Elizabethan to use to find out about Italy.'

▲ **SOURCE B:** The BBC's interpretation of an argument by David Kathman, an American scholar who edits a website about Shakespeare. Many Shakespeare plays are set in Italy.

'Shakespeare's name appeared on the very first printed editions of the works and other writers in his lifetime credit Shakespeare with being the author. Nobody ever claimed the plays were written by someone else during Shakespeare's lifetime.'

▲ **SOURCE C:** David Kathman, an American scholar who edits a website about Shakespeare.

'It is a bit strange that nothing is mentioned about his hometown yet 13 of his plays are set in Italy.'

▲ **SOURCE D:** William Leahy, founder of a university course on Shakespeare Authorship Studies, Brunel University.

'There are no official records that state Shakespeare was a writer, but there are about 70 documents that state he was an actor or a money-lender. There are only six examples of his signature – and they all spell his name differently.'

▲ **SOURCE E:** William Leahy, founder of a university course on Shakespeare Authorship Studies, Brunel University.

'The idea that [Shakespeare] was a poor man and a commoner is wrong. His father was the mayor of Stratford, which was a thriving market town. He came from a decent background and his education at Stratford Grammar School rivalled any education today.'

▲ **SOURCE F:** Stuart Hampton-Reeves, of the British Shakespeare Association.

'Shakespeare could have gone to Stratford Grammar School but no records exist to prove that and, even if he did, it would have been only for six years.'

▲ **SOURCE G:** The BBC's interpretation of an argument by William Leahy, founder of a university course on Shakespeare Authorship Studies, Brunel University.

> 'William Shakespeare of Stratford-upon-Avon was an actor in the company that performed the plays of William Shakespeare, and was also a sharer in the theatre in which the plays were presented. To anyone with a logical mind, it follows that this William Shakespeare of Stratford-upon-Avon was also the writer of the plays and poems that bear his name. He is the man with the right name, at the right time and at the right place.'

Who was it, then?

Over the years, people have claimed that a number of different people were the real genius behind Shakespeare's plays. Today, most anti-Stratfordians believe that the works were written by Edward de Vere, who lived from 1550 to 1604. He was a nobleman who had two university degrees by the time he was 17, travelled widely and was famed for his poems even though none were published in his name. According to anti-Stratfordians, he was unable to publish plays in his own name as many of the characters were based on real people in Elizabeth's court, including the queen herself! If the plays were published under a false name, like William Shakespeare, no one could put the blame on de Vere!

▼ **SOURCE K:** *Matthew Cossolotto, former President of the Shakespeare Oxford Society.*

> 'Many of the plays contain characters and details that relate directly to De Vere's life. They show an intimate knowledge of a wide range of subjects, including the law, Italy, foreign languages, heraldry, music, navigation, court manners and gossip, and warfare. De Vere's known educational background, foreign travels and life experiences match the knowledge base shown in Shakespeare's plays and poems.'

◀ **SOURCE H:** *David Kathman, an American scholar who edits a website about Shakespeare.*

> 'Shakespeare returned to Stratford in his 40s, bought a big house, traded in grain and property and died in 1616. There was no large funeral, no commemoration in London and no poems written in his honour. He didn't leave a single book in his will and his daughters lived and died illiterate (unable to read or write).'

▲ **SOURCE I:** *Matthew Cossolotto, former President of the Shakespeare Oxford Society.*

> 'I am almost convinced that the assumed name [William Shakespeare] conceals the personality of Edward de Vere, Earl of Oxford. The man of Stratford seems to have nothing at all to justify his claim, whereas Oxford has almost everything.'

▲ **SOURCE L:** *Sigmund Freud, the world-famous psychologist.*

Wise Up Words

anti-Stratfordian   Stratfordian

Work

1 What is a:
   a Stratfordian?
   b anti-Stratfordian?

2 Write a brief description of each source in the correct column. Try to say why you've put the source in the column you've chosen.

Stratfordian	Anti-Stratfordian

3 Are you a Stratfordian or an anti-Stratfordian? Write a paragraph explaining your decision.

4 Do you think it matters if Shakespeare of Stratford was the true author of the works of Shakespeare? Give reasons for your answer.

◀ **SOURCE J:** *This bust of Shakespeare was placed in Holy Trinity Church, Stratford six years after Shakespeare's death. Anti-Stratfordians have claimed that it was only after his death that Shakespeare was thought of as a playwright. The final two lines on Shakespeare's grave say 'Blest be the man who spares these stones, and curst be he that moves my bones.' Some people have questioned whether this was meant to stop people investigating further.*

▼ **SOURCE M:** *Stuart Hampton-Reeves, of the British Shakespeare Association.*

> 'Where's the document that links De Vere or anyone else to the plays? It's non-existent.'

Fashion victims

The modern cosmetics industry is big business: shops and the media offer us thousands of products to make us look healthier, younger and more attractive. Things were different in Tudor times but rich women in particular still wanted to look their best. Many women made their own cosmetics, often with disastrous effects.

Mission Objectives

- Describe what some rich Tudor women did to their skin to create the 'perfect face' and why.

To be considered beautiful and wealthy, a Tudor woman needed pure white skin, ruby red lips, rosy cheeks, bright eyes and fair hair. A rich woman wanted white skin because she didn't want anyone to think that she needed to spend any time outside working and getting a tanned face. And as you will find out, Tudor women did many things to gain the 'perfect face'.

Today, many women (and men) suffer to make themselves look good. However, all our modern day suffering doesn't compare to the pain a Tudor woman must have gone through. She really was a fashion victim!

Eyes: Eyes had to be large and shining.

Solution: Put a chemical in them called **belladonna**.

Before

Hair: This must be light in colour.

Solution: Bleach with a mixture of sulphur and lead.

Face/neck: These had to be very white.

Solution: Drink rosewater and ass's milk in the evening. A mixture of white lead and vinegar would cause the skin to whiten in the day. Wear a mask when outside to prevent the sun causing freckles. Cover face with sublimate of mercury.

Eyebrows: These had to be very thin.

Solution: Pluck them out and paint on thin lines.

ASS'S MILK & ROSEWATER

WHITE LEAD POISON

Lips/cheeks: Lips had to be bright red, perhaps with matching red cheeks (to look like she was blushing).

Solution: **Cochineal** (crushed beetles) mixed with egg. Rub alum on the flesh to roughen up the skin. This would make the dye hold.

Teeth: These had to be very white.

Solution: Clean them with the frayed end of a stick dipped in brick dust and honey.

If the face was badly marked, sublimate of mercury took off the top layer of skin.

MERCURY POISON

After

Hair: Bleaching with sulphur and lead would cause the hair to fall out. Until that happened, a woman would pile her hair on top of her head. It would have been full of lice and other vermin because she rarely washed it.

Teeth: Most women over the age of 20 had smelly mouths, full of black teeth. As well as removing stains, the brick dust removed the enamel on the teeth, leaving them prone to decay.

Lips/cheeks: Cochineal was one of the safest substances used (we still use it today in cake icing – enjoy!). Alum, however, made the skin very rough and scarred.

Eyes: Belladonna was made from Deadly Nightshade (a plant), which is extremely poisonous and damaged the eyes of the user. It fogged their vision so they couldn't see properly.

Face/neck: White lead was extremely poisonous. It caused women to have wrinkles and, even worse, open sores that didn't heal. A lotion made from mercury (a silvery liquid metal) was also used. It is a very nasty chemical. It caused women's skin to peel like flaking paint. They hoped that the new layer of skin underneath, which would have been very painful to touch, would be whiter than the last.

FACT!

The Tudors thought bathing was unhealthy and very rarely washed. Even Queen Elizabeth, who was regarded as being extremely clean, bathed only every few weeks. No wonder people carried scented items around with them and wore lots of expensive perfume **imported** from the East. What a stink!

Work

1 a Listed below are some chemicals and substances that Tudor women used. Write them out in your book. Next to each one, write down what each was used for. For example: Belladonna – a chemical made from Deadly Nightshade, used to make Tudor women's eyes shine.
       • belladonna • cochineal • white lead • brick dust • sulphur • mercury
    b Now write down the effects each had on a Tudor woman's face.

2 Why did a rich Tudor woman want white skin?

3 a Using a full page in your book, draw the outline of a woman's face. Around the face, make a brief note of five points of advice to a Tudor fashion victim. Add the title 'How to avoid being a Tudor fashion victim'.
    b Using another full page, draw the outline of the face of a modern girl or boy. Around the face, make notes of your advice to a modern fashion victim. Add the title 'How to avoid being a modern fashion victim'.
    c What are the main differences between the way we look after our faces and the way they did in Tudor times? Think carefully. Are there any similarities?

Wise Up Words

belladonna   cochineal   imported

Be a Top Historian

Over many years, some things **change** a lot, while others change very little. As a top historian, you can see that the way people look after their faces has changed a lot… but there are some things that people do to their faces that have **stayed the same** since Tudor times.

Hungry for More?

Imagine you are an older Tudor woman whose face has suffered after years of damage from her strict 'beauty' regime. Design a warning leaflet to hand out to younger girls, outlining the dangers of all the terrible treatments.

Come dine with me!

Most of us get up around the same time – probably between 6:30 and 8:00am. We eat lunch and dinner at similar times and probably go to bed around the same time as well. We tend to call this our **routine** – a well-established pattern of behaviour we follow almost all the time.

There are other things in our lives that most of us do too. We eat similar things, drink similar things and even get our food from similar places. So what routines did people follow in Tudor times? Did daily life differ between rich and poor? And how did things change after the Tudors?

Mission Objectives

- Investigate how and why our modern daily routine differs from that of people in Tudor times.

Simple meals for country workers

In Tudor times, the average country worker got up just before sunrise and worked until 4:00 or 5:00 in the afternoon. At busy times of the year, such as harvest time, work would go on later, with men, women and children working in the fields until it was too dark to see. Workers would stop a couple of times each day for a break, eating a breakfast of bread and ale at 7:00am and a lunch of bread, cheese and beer (known as ale) around 11:00am.

The main meal of the day was eaten around 6:00pm when the workers came in from the fields. They usually ate a kind of stew (called pottage), which was almost entirely made up of vegetables such as turnips, cabbages, parsnips, onions, carrots and peas. They had bread (again) with this because the poor ate very little meat. Sometimes they caught rabbits or fish, or had a breast of chicken or bacon, but it was only the rich who could afford to buy (or hunt for) meat.

Fine dining for the rich

The rich got up early too, between 5:00 and 6:00am, and ate breakfast around 7:00am. Like the ordinary country workers, breakfast would consist of bread and ale, but a rich family's breakfast table might include meat or fish too.

Dinner time was around 12 noon and consisted of lots of courses, served one after the other. Beef, pork, mutton and fish, would be offered, but more unusual foods such as roasted pigeon, seagulls, lobster and peacock might appear as well. Salads and fruit pies were common, all washed down with ale, wine, sherry (or 'sack') and cider. Food was eaten with a spoon and a sharp pointed knife but by 1620 some people had started to use forks – some with eight prongs! Supper, consisting of the same sorts of food and drink as dinner, might also be eaten in the late afternoon or early evening.

FACT!

The name we give to 12 noon is 'midday', a shorter version of 'middle of the day'. But have you ever thought that 12 o'clock midday is not really the middle of the day in today's world at all? Nowadays, most adults get up around 7:00am (five hours before midday) and go to bed at 11:00pm (eleven hours after midday). In fact, the real middle of the day for most people today is around 3:00pm.

'The first course at dinner: pottage or stew, boiled meat or stewed meat. Chicken and bacon, powdered [finely chopped] beef pies, goose, pig, roasted beef, roasted veal, custard. The second course at dinner: roasted lamb, roasted capons [chickens], roasted conies [rabbits], chickens, peahens, baked venison, tart.'

▲ **SOURCE A:** *On this menu from 1575 for a well-off family, note that there are very few vegetables in their daily diet.*

What Happened When? 1650

In the mid-1600s, the three most common hot drinks – tea, coffee and cocoa – were introduced. Cocoa from Mexico, coffee from Arabia and tea from China.

SOURCE B: *A wealthy Tudor family enjoy their dinner.*

Key

1 Stone paving slabs covered the floor; rushes were scattered over them to make it more comfortable

2 Walls were plastered, but a large painted cloth or tapestry was often hung over them.

3 The trestle table is covered by a tablecloth

4 Two carved chairs for mother and father – sometimes cushions were added for comfort

5 Stools or benches for the children

6 An oak chest sometimes contained valuable family items like silver candlesticks or gold plates

7 Some of the plates were made from thick pottery or pewter made from tin and lead; in richer families the plates might be made from silver

8 Spoons and knives were used but diners still ate much of their food with their fingers; forks were rarely used until the mid 1600s

9 A rushlight, made from rushes soaked in grease; it burned very slowly

10 Ale was the main drink; drinking glasses began to appear in the sixteenth century, usually imported from Italy

11 Hot meat pies

12 Cheese

13 Pickled herrings

14 Roast pigeon

15 Roast beef

16 Apple pie

17 Leg of mutton

18 Bread

19 Fish plate containing pike, eels, salmon and carp

- Do not make faces at the table.
- Do not shout.
- Do not fill your mouth too full.
- Do not scratch your head with your fingers when you are eating meat.
- Do not blow on your food to cool it.
- Do not blow out crumbs when you eat.
- Do not take all the best food for yourself.
- Do not gulp down drink too fast.
- Do not pick your teeth with your knife.
- Do not spit out food.

Work

1 a What is meant by the term 'daily routine'?

 b In what ways was the daily routine of the rich similar to that of poorer country workers in Tudor times?

 c In what ways were their routines different?

 d How is your daily routine different from, or similar to, that of people in Tudor times?

2 Imagine you've been invited to go for a meal at the home shown in **Source B**. Describe what it's like and what you ate. Take time to describe the room as well as the meal. Use **Source C** to help you, too.

◀ **SOURCE C:** *Tudor table manners. These top tips for table behaviour appeared in a Tudor book in 1577. Most of us learned some of these manners when we were young!*

The topic of crime and punishment is big news. The latest crime figures, the nastiest murder trials and the state of our prisons are issues that are always on our television screens, on the radio and in newspapers and magazines. As a result, we know quite a lot about law and order in today's society. But what was the state of law and order in Tudor times? What types of criminals roamed the country? And how were these criminals caught and punished?

Mission Objectives

- Investigate how some of the poorer people in Tudor times tried to make money.
- Explain why these so-called 'sturdy beggars' were treated so brutally.
- Judge how well Tudor society dealt with the poor.

The origin of the 'sturdy beggar'

The number of poor people increased in Tudor times. The first Tudor king, Henry VII, banned his rich barons from keeping private armies, so lots of men lost their jobs as soldiers. To make matters worse, many large landowners started to keep sheep on their land rather than allow farmers to rent it and grow crops. This meant fewer jobs, so farmers and their workers and families had to leave the manors to fend for themselves. Later, when Henry VIII closed all the monasteries, the increasing number of poor people couldn't even go to the local monks for their handouts.

All this led to an increase in the number of poor people wandering the streets and looking for food and shelter. These **vagabonds**, as the Tudors called them, were a mixture of unemployed soldiers and farmers, women and children, and the old and sick. A small minority, who were fit enough to look for work, found that crime was an easier way for them to make a living. These rough, tough, devious vagabond conmen were also known as '**sturdy beggars**'.

Different types of sturdy beggar

In about 1567, a man named Thomas Harman wrote a best-selling book warning against the dangers of sturdy beggars. He described 23 different types of tricksters, some of whom are detailed here.

Bristler

The Bristler would use specially weighted dice ('bristles' were loaded or crooked dice), which would land on whichever number the Bristler chose, in order to cheat at gambling.

Counterfeit crank

Dressed in old, grubby clothes, he would pretend to have violent fits. He would often suck soap so that he frothed at the mouth! The more he shook, the more money he hoped to attract from people who felt sorry for him.

The Clapper Dudgeon

He would cut his skin to make it bleed and tie dirty rags over the wounds to make them look even worse. He hoped people would feel sorry for him and give him money for 'medical attention'.

Wise Up Words

canting   House of Correction   sturdy beggar   vagabond

Tom O'Bedlam

He would pretend to be mad and follow people around. Often he would carry a stick with a piece of meat attached to the end or spend hours barking like a dog or stuffing chicken heads into his ears. Why do you think people gave him money?

FACT!

In 1566, London beggar Nicholas Jennings was caught with a bag of blood that he used to paint fake injuries on his head. In a day he made the equivalent of two weeks' wages for an ordinary worker.

The Baretop Trickster

These women would trick men into buying them a meal, having taken off some of their clothes. Perhaps the man thought he would get more than food – and he usually did! He would be robbed and beaten by the woman and her gang of thieves.

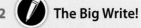

SOURCE A: *This picture of baretop tricksters appeared in a warning leaflet in the 1500s.*

Work

1 a Why did the number of poor people increase in Tudor times?

  b What was a 'sturdy beggar'?

2   **The Big Write!**

The year is 1543 and you work as a printer in a large town. The mayor has asked you to design a leaflet warning visitors about the dangers of sturdy beggars. Your warning leaflet should include details about some (or all) of the sturdy beggars mentioned on these pages and about how they might try to trick someone.

Cutpurse – a pickpocket who would creep up behind you, cut a hole in your pocket or bag and steal the contents.

Angler – fixed a hook to a long stick and stole clothes from washing lines.

Dummerer – pretended to be deaf and dumb, hoping people would feel sorry for him.

Priggers of prancers – horse thieves.

Rufflers – ex-soldiers who beat people up to get their purses.

▲ **SOURCE A:** *These other sturdy beggars were featured in Harman's book about them, which was written in about 1567.*

FACT!

Sturdy beggars developed their own language, a kind of slang known as **canting**. They used it to speak secretly to other thieves on busy streets. Amazingly, some 'canting' words managed to work their way into everyday use. For example, booze (meaning 'alcohol'), peck (meaning 'food' – ever said you were 'peckish'?), duds (meaning 'clothes'), lift (meaning 'steal') and beak (meaning 'police' or the 'law') will still be recognizable to some of you today!

▼ **SOURCE B:** *Adapted from William Harrison's* Description of England, *published in 1587.*

'The vagabonds abide nowhere but run up and down from place to place… Idle beggars cut the fleshy parts of their bodies… to raise pitiful sores and move the hearts of passers-by so they will bestow large gifts upon them. How liberally they beg, what forcible speech… that makes me think that punishment is more suitable for them than generosity or gifts…

They are all thieves… They take from the godly poor what is due to them. It is not yet 60 years since this trade began but how it has prospered since that time is easy to judge for they are now supposed to amount to 10,000. Moreover, they have devised a language among themselves which they name "canting" such as none but themselves are able to understand.'

As the number of sturdy beggars increased, they became one of the country's biggest headaches. They were thought to be behind all sorts of crime and, in 1531, the government took firm action.

Whilst some old and sick people were given a special licence to beg, those who weren't given one would be whipped until their 'bodies be bloody' if they were caught out on the streets. If they were caught again, they had a 2.5cm hole bored through the ear, whilst a third conviction meant death by hanging! At one point, during Edward VI's reign, any person found begging even once would be made a slave for two years and branded on the forehead with the letter V for vagabond!

Gradually, it became clear that most vagabonds were not a threat to law and order at all. Instead, they were just genuinely poor and unemployed people who were looking for work. In the late 1500s, various laws were passed that ordered each district or parish to provide money for the poor. Queen Elizabeth I went one step further in 1601 when she backed the first official Poor Law. This said that each area should tax wealthy local people and use the money to provide work and support for the old and sick. The law still maintained that anyone who refused to work should be whipped and then put in a **House of Correction**. Even their children were taken from them and given jobs. Not surprisingly, some beggars were so afraid of the House of Correction that some areas reported a drop of 90 per cent in the number of people wandering the streets!

'29 March 1574. At Harrow on the Hill in Middlesex, on the said day, John Allen, Elizabeth Turner, Humfrey Foxe, Henry Bower and Agnes Wort, being over 14 years and having no lawful means of livelihood, were declared vagabonds… Sentenced to be flogged and burned through the right ear.'

▲ **SOURCE C:** *From Middlesex County Records, 1574.*

FACT!

There were prisons in Tudor and Stuart times but they tended to be places where people were held before their trial or while awaiting punishment. Unlike today, they were very rarely used as a punishment in their own right.

SOURCE D: *This table shows how the Tudors treated sturdy beggars.*

Date of law	King or queen	Action
1495	Henry VII	Beggars went in stocks (pictured here) for three days, then sent back to their birth place or previous residence.
1531	Henry VIII	Some 'worthy' poor, old and sick were given a licence to beg. Others were whipped and sent back to where they came from. Harsher punishments for repeat offenders.
1547	Edward VI	Beggars whipped and branded with a V (for vagabond) on forehead. Also made a slave for two years. If they offended again or tried to escape, they were executed (this law remained in force for three years before it was changed back to the 1531 law because it was viewed as too severe).
1601	Elizabeth I	Local taxes used to help the poor. Poor people who refused to work were imprisoned. Beggars were still whipped until they bled, and sent back to where they came from.

SOURCE E: *A beggar is whipped through the streets in 1567.*

FACT!

Some offences were dealt with by a local magistrate (trials for less serious crimes are still held in magistrates' courts today). Most guilty people were either fined or faced some sort of public humiliation, such as the stocks. Criminals accused of more serious crimes were often sent to a local jail until one of the king's (or queen's) judges visited a local large town and the trial could go ahead. At the trial, the prisoner had to conduct their own defence in front of the judge and jury.

Work

1. **a** Write down three examples of how sturdy beggars were punished if caught.
   b Why do you think Tudor kings and queens treated sturdy beggars so brutally?

2. Look at **Source B**.
   a Which type of sturdy beggar does the writer refer to in the first paragraph?
   b In the second paragraph, the writer says that sturdy beggars have 'devised a language'. What was this language called?
   c Why do you think sturdy beggars created their own words?

3. Look at **Source D**. In what ways did the Poor Law of 1601 differ from earlier laws that dealt with poor people?

4. **a** Here are five ways that sturdy beggars were punished: whipped, branded, hanged, put in a House of Correction, made into a slave. Write down the one you think was the most suitable punishment and explain why you chose it.
   b Why do you think we do not punish poor people and beggars today?

What did the Scottish boot, the Judas cradle and the Spanish donkey have in common?

In Tudor and Stuart times, crimes were punished in much the same way as they had been in the Middle Ages. The stocks and pillory were still used regularly but fining a criminal was still the most common way of punishing minor crimes. For serious offences, there were still very harsh punishments. In 1532, a cook was boiled to death in a cauldron for trying to poison the Bishop of Rochester (judges were perhaps trying to make the punishment fit the crime!).

Mission Objectives

- Analyse why and how torture was used during the Tudor and Stuart period.

Some towns had groups of men known as watchmen or constables to look out for crooks. Men called justices of the peace tried to investigate crimes, gather information and hold trials. However, these government-appointed men were also busy with other duties, such as looking after roads and bridges, checking alehouses and reporting people who continually failed to attend church! As a result, the government sometimes used other ways of getting information, catching criminals and foiling plots. One way was to employ spies but this was time-consuming and costly (you had to pay the spy, of course). A much more brutal solution was to use torture! So what were some of the more barbaric torture techniques?

The rack

How did it work?

A prisoner was stretched for hours on end. Often, their tendons and ligaments would tear and their shoulders would become dislocated.

Fact: There was only one rack in the whole of England, which was kept in the Tower of London. One famous Tudor rack torturer boasted that most of his victims were a foot longer by the time he had finished with them.

The press

How did it work?

A prisoner would lie under strong wooden or metal boards whilst heavy stones were placed upon them. If a prisoner failed to own up to their crimes, another heavy rock would be placed on them.

Fact: One press operator once boasted that he knew his victim would not be able to hold out much longer 'as soon as I heard his chest crack'.

The Spanish donkey

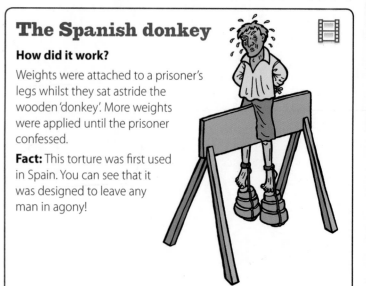

How did it work?

Weights were attached to a prisoner's legs whilst they sat astride the wooden 'donkey'. More weights were applied until the prisoner confessed.

Fact: This torture was first used in Spain. You can see that it was designed to leave any man in agony!

The Judas cradle

How did it work?

A victim was hung above a cone pyramid and then lowered onto it. The sharp tip of the cone was forced up between the prisoner's legs.

Fact: Today, when visitors are told about this torture on tours of the Tower of London, it usually gets the biggest gasps!

The Scottish boot

How did it work?

A prisoner's foot was placed in a heavy metal boot and wooden wedges would be hammered down the sides. Gradually, the leg and anklebones would be crushed and splintered into pieces.

Fact: A similar contraption called the copper boot was sometimes used. For this torture, molten red-hot lead was poured into a boot, giving the victim terrible burns.

Skeffington's Irons

How did it work?

These were specially designed to keep the prisoner in a very uncomfortable position. Either they owned up to the crime… or their back was broken.

Fact: This torture was named after its inventor, Leonard Skeffington, who was once head torturer for Henry VIII.

'They led me to a great upright beam or pillar of wood… At the top of it were iron staples for supporting weights. They placed on my wrists gauntlets [gloves] of iron, and ordered me to climb two or three steps. Then they raised my arms and inserted an iron bar through the rings of the gauntlets and then through the staples in the pillar, putting a pin through the bar so that it could not slip. When my arms were above my head, they withdrew the steps, one by one, from beneath my feet, so that I hung by my hands. The tips of my toes, however, still touched the ground, so they dug away the ground beneath… I began to pray, while the gentlemen standing round asked me if I was willing to confess.'

▲ **SOURCE A:** *Father Gerard, a Catholic priest, was tortured in the Tower of London in 1597.*

Be a Top Historian

Top historians are able to carry out **independent research**. Why not choose one of these instruments of torture and research it in detail. Or you could find out about other methods of torture that were used in the past.

Work

1 a What were the two main methods used to get information in Tudor times?

   b Why did the Tudors favour torture over the use of spies?

   c Do you think that torture was a good way to find out whether or not a person was guilty? Why or why not?

   d List as many reasons as you can to explain why we don't torture suspected criminals today.

2 Look at **Source A**.

   a In your own words, describe how Father Gerard was being tortured.

   b Why did earth have to be dug away from under the prisoner's feet?

3 **The Big Write!**

Most of this torture equipment still survives today, kept on display in the Tower of London. Design an information leaflet for a young schoolchild to use as a guide on a torture chamber tour. Include:

- colourful pictures of the torture instruments
- facts about how they worked
- background information on torture
- an imaginative title, for example, 'The Tower's Terrible Torture Guide'.

4.1A How did Britain build an empire?

Britain once controlled more countries and ruled over more people than any other nation in the world… ever! In 1900, for example, Britain ruled over 450 million people living in 56 different places all over the world. This amounted to a quarter of the world's population and a quarter of the Earth's total land area! All this land was known as the British Empire… and it all started on 5 March 1496 when the first Tudor king, Henry VII, ruled the country. So what exactly happened on that date? And how does it link to Britain having the largest empire the world has ever known?

Mission Objectives

- Explore how and why the British Empire began.
- Examine the significance of key individuals in the growth of the British Empire.

Age of discovery

In the late 1400s, explorers from Spain and Portugal made some dramatic discoveries. **Sources A** and **B** show some of them.

In 1492, an Italian explorer named Christopher Columbus (who was working for the Spanish) set sail across the Atlantic Ocean hoping to find new routes to India and China by sea. Instead, he discovered the West Indies, which Europeans didn't know existed! He sailed back several times and found more places. (See **Source A**.)

Vasco da Gama, from Portugal, was the first European to find a new route to India by sea. (Columbus didn't actually reach India, remember!) Da Gama sailed around the bottom of Africa and up the other side. (See **Source B**.)

SOURCE A: *Christopher Columbus' journey in 1492.*

SOURCE B: *Vasco da Gama's journey.*

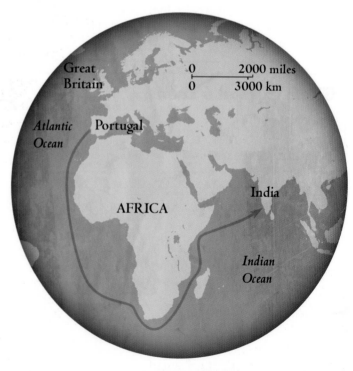

Here comes Henry!

In 1496, England joined the age of exploration when King Henry VII gave an Italian explorer called John Cabot the mission of finding new lands. (See **Sources C** and **D**.)

New found land

In 1497, Cabot sailed westwards from the port of Bristol across the Atlantic Ocean. A few months later, he landed on the coast of North America in what we now call Canada. He named it Newfoundland (for obvious reasons!), which the area is still called today. (See **Source E**.)

But there were no great riches to be found in this newly discovered place – no silks, no spices and no gold! So Cabot came home. However, this brief visit was the start of the British Empire. The British had claimed this land and intended to keep it. Over time, British settlers would move out to live in Newfoundland and eventually settle all along the east coast of what would become known as North America. In fact, the age of British people travelling abroad and taking land to live on had arrived!

SOURCE C: *John Cabot set out to find Asia and instead found North America.*

'You have free and full authority to sail to all parts and countries of the East, West and North under our flags with five ships and as many sailors as they can hold to seek, discover and find whatever islands, countries, regions or provinces of the heathens and infidels, whoever they may be and in what part of the world they be, which before this time have been unknown to all Christians.'

◀ **SOURCE D**: *Henry VII gave these orders to John Cabot on 5 March 1496. At the time, 'heathens' and 'infidels' referred to non-Christians.*

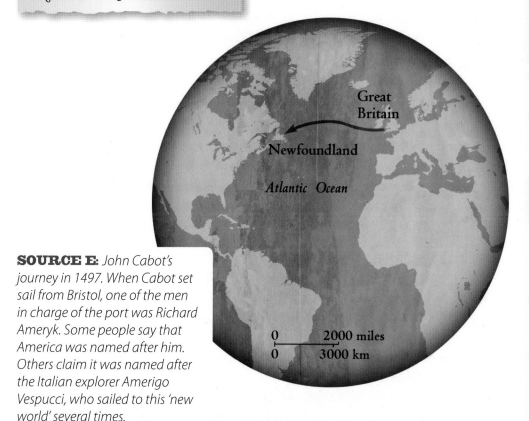

SOURCE E: *John Cabot's journey in 1497. When Cabot set sail from Bristol, one of the men in charge of the port was Richard Ameryk. Some people say that America was named after him. Others claim it was named after the Italian explorer Amerigo Vespucci, who sailed to this 'new world' several times.*

Work

1 a What is meant by the word 'empire'?
   b Why do many people think that 5 March 1496 was the day that the British Empire began?

2 Look at **Source D**.
   a Why do you think Henry VII was so keen to find new lands?
   b Did it matter whether any of the land Cabot found was inhabited or not? Explain your answer.
   c What does Henry VII's order tell us about his attitude? Give reasons for your answer.

3 a Explain what is meant by the word 'significant'.
   b How were Columbus, Henry VII and Cabot significant in the creation of the British Empire?

A false start?

John Cabot and his sailors didn't stay long in the 'new found land' of North America. They were short of supplies and wanted to get back home. In fact, no British settlers followed in Cabot's steps and went to live there for many years. When Henry VII died, his son Henry VIII did little to encourage people to revisit North America either. Neither did Edward VI, nor Mary I. They were clearly proud of the land that had been found in the New World (and felt it belonged to them), but didn't send people to live there. However, all that changed when Elizabeth I (Henry VII's granddaughter) became queen. She was *very* interested in exploring the world!

Go Gilbert go!

In 1578, Queen Elizabeth gave permission to an explorer called Humphrey Gilbert to travel to North America and build a settlement (known as a **colony**). The settlers hoped to farm, fish and perhaps find gold. Gilbert claimed hundreds of miles of land for the queen… but the settlers gave up and came home! Today, however, the area around where Gilbert landed is regarded as the first part of the British Empire. (See **Sources A** and **B**.)

New World Walter

In 1584, Queen Elizabeth sent another explorer called Walter Raleigh over to North America to set up another settlement. But this failed too because the settlers struggled to grow crops. However, in 1607, when King James I was on the throne, a group of settlers *did* manage to survive out in the New World and start new lives. They built homes and grew new crops like tobacco, sugar and cotton, which they sold back to Britain and made lots of money. Before long, there were hundreds of British people living in North America, trying to make money and start a new life.

Money, money, money

Soon, British businessmen (or traders) realized that if they bought popular items abroad, where they were cheap, and brought them back to Britain, they could be sold for high prices. So traders travelled all over the world to get exotic spices, luxury cloth and goods like sugar, tea, coffee, and fur. Then they brought them back to Britain and made a fortune selling them. Sometimes the traders might build a huge trading station in the foreign land to keep themselves safe… and often took lots of land around it.

SOURCE A: *Sir Humphrey Gilbert cuts the soil in Newfoundland in August 1583. The ceremony symbolized that the land was now English. The natives had no say in the matter!*

SOURCE B: *This plaque commemorates the place in North America where Gilbert claimed land for Queen Elizabeth.*

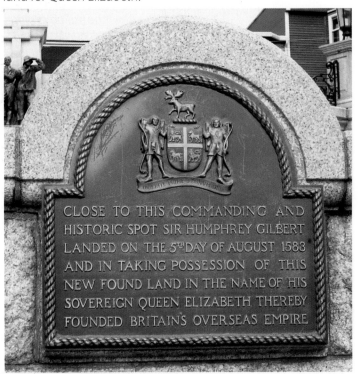

CLOSE TO THIS COMMANDING AND HISTORIC SPOT SIR HUMPHREY GILBERT LANDED ON THE 5TH DAY OF AUGUST 1583 AND IN TAKING POSSESSION OF THIS NEW FOUND LAND IN THE NAME OF HIS SOVEREIGN QUEEN ELIZABETH THEREBY FOUNDED BRITAIN'S OVERSEAS EMPIRE

Fight, fight, fight!

Occasionally, the British would fight with a foreign power, like Spain or the Netherlands, and take some of their overseas land too. In 1665, for example, the British seized a town called New Amsterdam from the Dutch… and renamed it New York after King Charles II's brother, the Duke of York! So, as a result of gaining land by either winning it or taking it, Britain managed to get control of several different areas in various parts of the world (see **Source C**). Over the next 200 years, this British Empire would grow to become the largest the world had ever known!

What Happened When?

1607

In 1607, the same year that the first successful British colony in America was founded, 'God Save the King' was first sung. It was performed at a banquet given to celebrate James I's escape from the Gunpowder Plot.

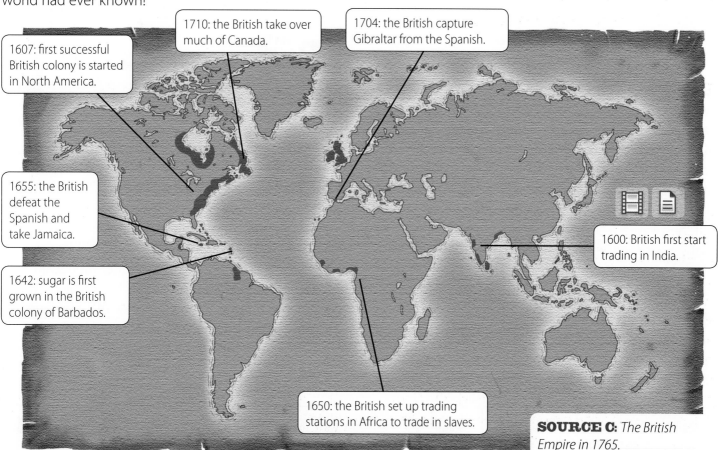

1710: the British take over much of Canada.

1704: the British capture Gibraltar from the Spanish.

1607: first successful British colony is started in North America.

1655: the British defeat the Spanish and take Jamaica.

1600: British first start trading in India.

1642: sugar is first grown in the British colony of Barbados.

1650: the British set up trading stations in Africa to trade in slaves.

SOURCE C: *The British Empire in 1765.*

Work

1. Each of these dates is important in the early years of Britain's empire:

   1497; 1583; 1492; 1584; 1607; 1496; 1665; 1642; 1710; 1600; 1655.

   Write the dates in order. Beside each date, write what happened in that year. (You might have to turn back to pages 64 and 65 to find some of the dates.)

2. In your own words, explain how each of the following places got their names:

   • Newfoundland   • the New World   • New York

3. Explain how the following helped the British Empire to grow:

   • trade   • wars   • new crops

Be a Top Historian

The growth of Britain's empire had several **causes**. Top historians know that most events have a number of causes… and these causes can sometimes be **linked**. Can you link together any of the main causes of the growth of Britain's empire?

How was Britain involved in the slave trade?

The idea of slavery is a very old one. The Egyptians, for example, used slaves to build the pyramids and the Romans forced them to fight in gladiator arenas. But slaves were used in the Tudor and Stuart periods too, especially by countries that had started to take over the New World of North America, South America and the Caribbean. So where did the slaves come from? Why were they needed? And in what way was Britain involved?

Mission Objectives

- Recall why slaves were taken to the New World.
- Examine Britain's role in the slave trade.

Before reading any further, think about the word '**slave**'. Who or what was a slave? What does the word mean?

Using slaves

When people from countries like Spain, Portugal, France and Britain began to settle in the New World in the 1500s, they would often set up farms to grow crops such as sugar, cotton and tobacco. To begin with they might capture people from local tribes to use as slaves on the farms. But the supply of local tribes didn't last long. Disease and poor treatment soon wiped out many. So when the settlers ran out of local people to use as slaves, they decided to go somewhere else to find new ones – Africa!

A trade in slaves

African slaves were taken over to North America, South America and the Caribbean in a system known as the slave trade. **Source A** shows how it worked.

FACT!

On one Caribbean island, there were around two million native people when the Spanish took over in 1492. Sixty years later, there were none left!

The British get involved

The British got involved in the slave trade in 1562 when Sir John Hawkins got permission from Queen Elizabeth to transport captured slaves from Africa to America and sell them there. He made a fortune – and soon lots of British slave traders were doing it. In fact, by 1568 Hawkins was making so much money that he asked the queen if he could have a family coat of arms that included his new money-making scheme. Look carefully at **Source B** to see what was on his coat of arms.

Stage 1: A **slave trader** would leave Europe in a ship. It might be loaded with goods such as pots, pans, alcohol, guns and cloth.

Well, there she is!

The ship is full of goods that are cheap to buy in Europe, but highly prized in Africa.

Stage 2: The ship would sail to the African coast. The crew might land and kidnap local African men, women and children.

Stage 3: The ship's crew might meet with local African tribesmen and swap the goods in the ship for prisoners from other tribes who had already been captured to sell.

SOURCE A: *Businessmen made a fortune from the slave trade.*

Stage 4: Then the ship would sail to the New World and sell the slaves there.

Stage 5: The slaves were put to work. As well as farming, they might hunt animals, work in houses or dig for gold.

Stage 6: The ship might then be loaded with sugar, cotton or tobacco to take back to Europe… and sell for a huge profit.

We will make a fortune selling all this!

These goods are so popular in Europe now.

Hungry for More?

John Hawkins was also involved in British seafaring in other ways. Do some research to find out about what part he played in the English navy. You might want to investigate something called the 'Spanish Armada'.

Wise Up Words

slave   slave trader

SOURCE B: *John Hawkins' new coat of arms was granted in 1568.*

How many?

Official figures show that over 10,000 British ships took slaves over the Atlantic Ocean to the Americas and the Caribbean. Many British people played a significant part in this too – ship owners, slave traders and slave owners, for example. But there were many other Britons who were linked to slavery in other ways – dockworkers unloading ships full of cotton that slaves had grown, workers turning the cotton into shirts and even the shop owners selling sugar and tobacco.

Ports like Bristol and Liverpool grew into large cities during this time and many of their fine buildings, which still stand today, were built with the profits from slavery. Even Penny Lane, the street in Liverpool made famous by the Beatles song in 1967, is reputed to have been named after James Penny, the owner of a slave ship!

Work

1 Explain your ideas about what the word 'slave' means.

2 Why did European settlers in the Americas want slaves?

3 In your own words, explain how a slave trader might make money from the slave trade. Use **Source A** to help you. You might also want to create a diagram to help your explanation.

4 Look closely at **Source B**. How can you tell that John Hawkins was involved with the slave trade?

5 Today, we think the idea of slavery is wrong, although trade in human lives – people trafficking – does go on. John Hawkins and many like him saw nothing wrong with selling slaves. Why do you think opinions have changed so much?

Blackbeard: the original pirate of the Caribbean

In Tudor times, Spain became one of the richest countries in the world. Most of its riches came from gold found in the Americas, which was brought back to Spain on treasure ships. Queen Elizabeth was envious of Spain's wealth and encouraged her sailors to rob foreign ships. She gave ships' captains special permission to steal as much as they could… as long as they shared anything they stole with her! So who were these specially licenced sailors? How were they different from pirates? And who was the most famous pirate of all?

Mission Objectives

- Explain the difference between a pirate and a privateer.
- Explain why monarchs encouraged privateers.
- Recall key events in Blackbeard's life.

Privateer or pirate?

Any sailor with permission to attack foreign ships and steal from them was known as a **privateer**. Any sailor who didn't have permission, and kept the treasure all to themselves, was known as a **pirate**. Many pirates started out as privateers… but didn't want to share! Some pirates even robbed ships from their own nation. And one of those men became the most famous pirate of all – Blackbeard!

Edward 'Blackbeard' Teach

Born in Bristol in the late 1600s, Blackbeard's real name was Edward Teach. He was a huge man who realized that one of his main weapons was terror.

Blackbeard had once been a privateer, working for Anne, the Queen of Great Britain at the time. His main hunting grounds were the seas around the Caribbean islands of Jamaica, Barbados and St Kitts. But Blackbeard had become greedy and decided that he didn't want to share what he'd stolen, so he became a pirate instead. He captured a ship from the French and transformed it into his own pirate ship, the *Queen Anne's Revenge*. It was easily recognizable, due to his famous flag (see **Source B**.)

SOURCE A:
Blackbeard went to great lengths to look as terrifying as possible.

His hair was long and black.

He had a big, bushy black beard.

He stuck slow-burning matches into his hair and beard. Smoke curled around his face.

He carried six pistols in a belt strung over his hairy chest.

He also carried two swords and several daggers.

SOURCE B: *Blackbeard's pirate flag.*

Life on board a pirate ship

Being a member of Blackbeard's pirate crew was a risky business. Conditions on board ship were terrible – rats, fleas, mice, lice – and keeping food fresh was a constant problem. The pirates tended to live on salted beef or pork, fish, biscuits, and beer. Often their food went rotten, so they longed to capture a ship full of good things to eat.

> '*Blackbeard would kill a member of his crew now and then, just to remind the others who was boss. One captured crew member said, "If he did not now and then kill one of them, they would forget who he was".*'

▲ **SOURCE C:** *Written by a modern historian.*

Blackbeard's reign didn't last forever. Lieutenant Robert Maynard of the British Royal Navy was given the job of tracking him down. He spotted Blackbeard's ship on 21 November 1718. After a fierce ship battle in which Blackbeard was shot five times, stabbed 20 times and slashed across the throat, he was eventually killed. And because it was a custom of the time to display dead pirates as a warning to others, Maynard cut off Blackbeard's head and hung it up on the front of his ship until it rotted. The remaining crew members were hanged.

FACT!

According to legend, Blackbeard's skull was made into a cup soon after his death. Today there is a huge reward for anyone who can find it!

Wise Up Words

pirate   privateer

Injury	Payment
Loss of both legs	1500 pieces of eight or 15 slaves
Loss of both hands	1800 pieces of eight or 18 slaves
For one leg	600 pieces of eight or 6 slaves
For one hand	same as a leg
Loss of an eye	100 pieces of eight or 1 slave

▲ **SOURCE D:** *An agreement drawn up by pirates in case of injury.*

Work

1 In your own words, explain the difference between a pirate and a privateer.

2 Here are some key events in Blackbeard's life – but they are all mixed up! Write them out in the order in which they happened:
   - Captured the a French ship and renamed it *Queen Anne's Revenge*
   - Was shot, stabbed and slashed across the throat
   - Became a pirate
   - Born in Bristol in 1680
   - Robert Maynard was given the job of hunting him down
   - His head was displayed on Maynard's ship
   - Worked as a privateer for Queen Anne

3   **The Big Write!**

   Imagine you are one of Blackbeard's pirate crew. Write at least three diary entries that give details of your pirate life over the past few years. Remember to include:
   - the conventions of a diary, such as dates, using 'Dear Diary', and writing about how you feel. Look at page 122 for some examples of diary entries.
   - information about your boss, Blackbeard – what does he look like? Has he always been a pirate? How tough is he?
   - facts about the life of a pirate – what are conditions on board a ship like? What do you eat? Is it dangerous? How successful was Blackbeard's crew?
   - details about the hunt for Blackbeard – who hunted him? How was Blackbeard killed? What happened to his body? What might happen to you?

5.1 Young Elizabeth: what was she like?

In 1533, King Henry's second wife, Anne Boleyn, announced she was pregnant. The king desperately wanted a son who could be king after him. He already had one daughter, Mary, and he didn't want another one. He worried that a woman would never be clever enough or strong enough to run a country. On the 7 September 1533, Princess Elizabeth Tudor was born. Henry was very disappointed. He sulked for weeks and didn't even attend her christening!

Mission Objectives

- Investigate why Princess Elizabeth, King Henry VIII's youngest daughter, was such a clever student.
- Examine the circumstances in which she became queen.

Elizabeth was two years old when her mum was executed and over the next few years she would have four different stepmothers. Elizabeth never lived with her dad and was sent to live with her half-sister, Mary.

The girls had three houses: Hatfield and Eltham, near London, and Hunsdon House in Hertfordshire. When they travelled between each house, they would fight over who would walk at the front of the procession. It doesn't appear to have been an easy life for young Elizabeth: a dead mother, a tough father, an awkward half-sister and lots of stepmothers. And when her half-brother Edward was born, it didn't look like she would ever be queen!

But despite some difficulties in her life, Princess Elizabeth had one major factor in her favour – she was clever. In fact, by the time she was sixteen, she could speak five languages – English, French, Italian, Greek and Latin. So what was the secret of her success? Study the cartoons and the sources carefully. They outline how Elizabeth was such a clever young lady!

Secret of her success No. 1: she enjoyed learning.

Elizabeth had her own personal tutors and really enjoyed working hard at her lessons. It was very fashionable at the time for rich young women to be highly educated and Elizabeth loved writing poems, translating foreign books and learning new languages.

Secret of her success No. 2: she got attention because she was clever.

King Henry was disappointed when Elizabeth was born but soon grew to love spending time with his clever daughter. When Henry visited Elizabeth, her half-sister was probably very jealous. Mary was locked away in a separate room whilst the king and his youngest daughter chatted, swapped gifts and sang together.

Secret of her success No. 3: she was lonely.

Elizabeth didn't really have any real friends. But reading books and learning new skills meant that she could talk about them with people. People weren't going to voice their real opinions about the country to the king's daughter but they might be honest about their views on books, music and horses.

Secret of her success No. 4: there wasn't much else to do.

There was no television, radio or Internet in Tudor times. Books, music and horse riding provided entertainment for her – and she seemed to be very good at many of the things she tried.

Monday	Tuesday	Wednesday	Thursday	Friday
Bible study	Bible study	Bible study	Bible study	Bible study
Book translation: Greek to English	Book translation: English to Greek	Book translation: Latin to English	Book translation: English to Latin	Philosophy
Lunchtime – Food ~ Walking ~ Riding ~ Games				
French conversation	Italian conversation	Latin conversation	English conversation	Greek conversation
Philosophy	Book translation: Latin to English	Book translation: English to Latin	Book translation: Greek to English	Book translation: English to Greek

▲ **SOURCE A:** Elizabeth had a very full timetable when she was being taught by one of her tutors.

'She is most eager. Her mind has no womanly weakness; her perseverance is equal to that of a man and she has a long memory. She talks French and Italian as well as English, and has often talked to me in Latin and Greek. She has beautiful handwriting and is a skilful musician.'

◀ **SOURCE B:** Written by one of her tutors, Robert Ascham. Not a bad school report, is it?

Elizabeth was thirteen years old when her father died and her younger half-brother, Edward, became king (aged nine). Although she was quite close to Edward, many people suspected she might be plotting against him during his short reign (he died aged fifteen). However, nothing could ever be proved against her.

When her older half-sister, Mary, became queen in 1553, Elizabeth was again suspected of plotting against the monarch – and again nothing could be proved. To be on the safe side, Mary kept Elizabeth like a prisoner at various country houses.

Five years later, in 1558, whilst Elizabeth was (typically) sitting reading under a tree at Hatfield House, she received word that her sister, Queen Mary, was dead. Aged 25, Elizabeth was now Queen of England.

SOURCE C: In this painting Elizabeth was aged 13. Why do you think the artist included books in the picture?

Work

1 What difficulties did Elizabeth face in her early life?

2 Look closely at **Source A**.
   a Explain why you think the following subjects take up so much of Elizabeth's study time:
   • Bible study
   • conversation
   • learning and translating foreign languages.
   b Think of three subjects that you study at school today that are not on Elizabeth's timetable. Why do you think it is important that you study them?

3 Imagine that you are Princess Elizabeth's tutor. King Henry has asked you to write a school report about his daughter. It should include details about:
   • her lessons
   • her strengths
   • her attitude towards learning.
   Why don't you set it out like one of your school reports?

5.2 What did Queen Elizabeth look like?

Our current monarch is known to millions of people all over the world. Her face is on television, in the newspapers and even on the money we use. Some people have seen her in real life as she travels around Britain and the world. Her family life has even been made into films and television dramas. Many people today are fascinated by our royal family.

Mission Objectives

- Explore why it is so hard to establish what Queen Elizabeth really looked like.
- Examine why Elizabeth controlled her royal portraits so carefully.
- Compare a number of royal portraits and judge which one would be most suitable for the queen.

In the sixteenth century, ordinary people were also very interested in their queen – Elizabeth I. However, there was no television or daily newspapers to show what she looked like. You might have been lucky enough to glimpse her as she toured around but it was highly unlikely that an ordinary person would see her in the flesh.

In order for ordinary people to know what she looked like, Elizabeth used portraits. However, Elizabeth was a wise queen and she cleverly controlled pictures that the public saw in order to create an image of herself that would impress everyone. Lord Cecil, who worked for the queen, once said:

'Many painters have done portraits of the queen but none has shown her looks and charms. Therefore, she has asked people to stop doing portraits of her until a clever painter has finished one which all other painters can copy. Her Majesty, in the meantime, forbids the showing of any portraits which are ugly, until they are improved.'

The queen would have official portraits sent to artists to be copied. No other portraits were allowed. For years, the artist would copy these portraits every time an admirer wanted a portrait of the queen.

Look at the five portraits here (**Sources A** to **E**) and see if you can match them to the descriptions (1–5).

SOURCE A

SOURCE B

SOURCE C

Important visitors to England who met Elizabeth probably saw a very different person to the lady we see in the paintings. Some of the following comments are even quite insulting. We must remember that the queen was over 60 when they were written.

SOURCE D

SOURCE E

FACT!

Elizabeth sat down to be painted only eight times – but over 200 paintings of her exist today. This shows just how many times artists were instructed to copy other paintings.

'On her head she wears a great red wig... Her face appears to be very aged. It is long and thin. Her teeth are yellow and unequal and there are less on the left than on the right. Many of them are missing and one cannot understand her easily when she speaks quickly. She is tall and graceful.'

▲ **SOURCE A:** *A French visitor, 1597.*

'Her face is oblong, fair but wrinkled; her eyes small, yet black and pleasant; her nose is a little hooked; her lips narrow; and her teeth black... She wears false hair and that red... her hands are small, her fingers long and her height neither tall nor short.'

▲ **SOURCE F:** *A German visitor, 1598.*

Painting descriptions

1. Painted in 1588, just after the Spanish had tried, and failed, to invade England. In the background are wrecked Spanish ships. Elizabeth's hand is on a globe to show she is one of the most powerful people in the world.

2. Painted soon after she was crowned. Elizabeth was about 25 years old. Note the crown, the orb (ball) and the sceptre (long stick), which are symbols of power and authority. Also look at all the jewels and gold-coloured cloth used to show how wealthy she is.

3. An engraving of Elizabeth, created when she was in her fifties. Notice the 'bags' under her eyes.

4. Painted when she was in her sixties. Look carefully at her dress; it is covered in eyes and ears. What do you think the message is here?

5. Painted when Elizabeth was in her sixties. She is wearing a wig here.

Work

1. a Why would it be unlikely that an ordinary person would meet Elizabeth I?
   b Why, then, were portraits of the queen so important for Elizabeth and her subjects?

2. a Select one of the portraits on these pages. In your own words, write a detailed description of Elizabeth based on the picture.
   b If Elizabeth herself were to read your description, would she be pleased with what you have written? Explain your answer.
   c Which of the portraits (**Sources A** to **E**) do you think Elizabeth would be most pleased with? Explain your answer.

3. Explain why Elizabeth didn't allow 'the showing of any portraits which are ugly'.

4. Read **Sources F** and **G**.
   a Write down the details that both writers agree on.
   b Is there anything they disagree on?
   c Can you think of reasons why the writers might disagree?

5.3 Why did Queen Elizabeth kill her cousin?

By 1568, Elizabeth had been queen for ten years. She hadn't married and she hadn't any children. This meant that if she died, her cousin, Mary, Queen of Scotland, would become Queen of England and Wales too.

Mission Objectives

- Identify who Mary was and why she was heir to England's throne.
- Examine the threat posed by Mary, Queen of Scots.
- Investigate the Babington Plot.

Mary, Queen of Scotland, had a troubled past. She was known as a great beauty but had difficulty keeping her husbands! She was once married to the King of France, who died in a freak riding accident. She then married an English lord, who was strangled and blown up. Soon after this, she married the man who was suspected of murdering her second husband!

The Scots were suspicious of Mary's connection to her second husband's death and some rebelled against her. She was forced to give up her throne and stand aside as her young son James was made King of Scotland. In 1568, she ran away to England, perhaps hoping that her cousin, Queen Elizabeth, would take pity on her.

Mary immediately caused problems for Elizabeth. For a start, she was Catholic, and made no secret of the fact that she thought she should be Queen of England instead of Elizabeth. Some English Catholics even agreed with her. Elizabeth's solution was a harsh but typically clever one. She kept Mary a prisoner until she could make up her mind what to do with her. In fact, Mary was kept in various houses and castles and imprisoned for the next 19 years.

The two women never actually met each other during this time but, finally, Elizabeth was forced to take action against Mary when she discovered that Mary was involved in a plot to kill her!

SOURCE A: *This is the part of Mary's letter that led to her execution. Can you work out what she wrote? What does she mean?*

Babington's plot

In 1586, a young, rich Catholic man called Anthony Babington came up with a secret plan to kill Elizabeth. He would organize six men to kill the English queen, rescue Mary from her prison, and make her the new Queen of England. However, Babington needed to know if Mary liked the idea. He needed to contact her in prison.

Secret letters

He managed to get Mary's servants to hide secret letters in beer barrels that were taken to her room. The letters were written in code. Mary wrote back saying she agreed to the plan (see **Source A**). In fact, Mary's servants didn't work for her at all, they worked for England's chief spy, Sir Francis Walsingham, who took the letters straight to Elizabeth.

When the code was broken, the message was clear: Mary was supporting a plan to kill the queen. This was **treason**.

Killing her cousin

Despite all the evidence, Elizabeth still didn't want to have her cousin executed. Eventually, her secretary, William Davison, slipped the death warrant in among some papers she had to sign. Elizabeth pretended she didn't really know what she was signing, signed it, changed her mind, then tried to stop the execution. But she was too late. Mary, Queen of Scots, had already been executed (see **Source B**).

What Happened When?

1587

In the same year that Mary was executed, Virginia Dare was born. Virginia was the first child born in America to English parents. They had settled at the English colony of Roanoke just a few months before. No one knows what happened to Virginia (or her parents) because all the settlers disappeared!

SOURCE B: *The execution of Mary, Queen of Scots, in February 1587. Her pet dog went with her to her execution, hidden under her dress. The axeman took at least three blows to cut her head off. It was said that her lips continued to move after her head was separated from her body. Then her wig fell off!*

Wise Up Words

treason

5.4A Match of the day: England versus Spain

In Tudor times, Spain was the richest, most powerful country in the world. It had a huge army and Spanish treasure ships were bringing a fortune in gold back to Spain from newly discovered lands. But in 1588, Spain's King Philip II decided to focus all his country's great power and wealth on one thing – the invasion of England! He set every shipyard in Spain to work building what many described as the greatest navy – or **Armada** – ever created. This massive fleet of 130 huge warships was heading for one place – England!

So why was Philip so angry with the English? How was his ambitious invasion plan designed to work? And how successful were the Spanish when battle finally commenced in this world-famous 'match of the day'?

Mission Objectives

- Explore why the King of Spain decided to invade England in 1588.
- Compare the strengths and weaknesses of England and Spain's navies.
- Judge key reasons why the Spanish Armada failed.

Why was Philip so angry?

Few people had ever seen Philip II, King of Spain, so angry. It was the morning of 20 April 1587 and he had just received some shattering news. The most famous English explorer of all, Sir Francis Drake, had just sailed into Cadiz harbour in southern Spain and set fire to 30 of Spain's royal warships! Philip was furious but he had other reasons to be angry with the English.

- For years, the English sailors had been stealing gold and silver from Spanish ships.
- Philip (a Catholic) had recently heard news that Mary, Queen of Scots, (another Catholic) had been executed by Elizabeth I. He thought that the people who had killed a Catholic queen should be punished.
- At this time, the Spanish Netherlands (now known as Belgium and Luxembourg) were controlled by Spain. But many people who lived there didn't want this and rebelled against Spanish control. The rebels were being helped by soldiers from another country. Yes, you've guessed it – England!

Attack!

By the summer of 1588, Philip's forces had recovered from Drake's attack on Cadiz and Philip had assembled one of the greatest fleets of warships the world had ever seen. There were 130 Spanish ships, known as an Armada, many painted red and gold, which together covered an area of about 12km^2 of sea. Philip's aim for the fleet was simple – meet up with 20,000 ground troops at Calais, transport them to invade England and remove Elizabeth from the English throne. Philip would then become King of Spain and England.

NEXT FIXTURE

The English Navy
Owner: Queen Elizabeth

Managers: Lord Howard and Sir Francis Drake

Vs

The Spanish Armada
Owner: King Philip II

Manager: The Duke of Medina Sidonia

Date: Summer 1588
Venue: The English Channel

But England had a navy too, which was prepared to fight to the death to defend the country against the foreign invaders. Read the information on these pages carefully and judge how the two sides might match up against each other.

The Spanish have a fantastic fleet and they're confident that they will beat the English. They even call themselves the 'invincible Armada'. They do have a problem though. Their commander, the Duke of Medina Sidonia, suffers from seasickness. Can you believe that? A seasick sea captain!

SOURCE A: *This painting shows the Armada setting sail for England.*

Wise Up Words

Armada   beacon crescent   galleon   musket

Work

1 a Why did Philip decide to attack England in 1588?

b What was his plan if his invasion was a success?

2 a In your own words, describe how either an English or a Spanish ship's captain would try to defeat an enemy. You might wish to illustrate your answer.

b In your opinion, which fleet of ships, the English or the Spanish, stood the better chance of success? Explain your answer carefully.

PAIN

A Spanish galleon (on the left)

Number of ships: 7.5/10

Length of ships: 9/10

Mobility: 4/10

No. of sailors: 8.5/10

Weapons: 6/10

Ability of commanders: 3.5/10

The Spanish are 'ropers and raiders'. Their ships are like huge floating castles, but are clumsy to steer. So the Spanish **galleons** will try to sail alongside the enemy ships and tie themselves alongside with ropes and hooks. Then soldiers will jump onto the enemy ships and fight with swords, daggers and **muskets**. The heavy guns below decks will almost touch the other ships and will blow holes in their sides.

The English have a strong team — about 130 ships, but only 60 or so are fit to fight. The Spanish galleons are about 50 metres long, but the English ones are about half that length. As a result the English ships are much quicker. They have two other advantages: firstly, they have some of the most accurate long-range guns ever built, and secondly, most of them use the same standard size cannonball. Spanish ships have guns of different sizes and types, and finding the right size of cannonball for each gun during the heat of battle must be tricky!

ENGLAND

An English galleon (on the right)

No. of ships: 7.5/10

Length of ships: 5/10

Mobility: 7/10

No. of sailors: 8/10

Weapons: 9/10

Ability of commanders: 8.5/10

The English are 'speedy smashers'. Their experienced sailors should be able to avoid any enemy attempts to get alongside. Instead, they will hope to position their ships 150m away and use their superior guns to fire huge solid 20kg cannonballs through the side of the enemy ships. Then the smaller cannons known as 'man killers' will fire 8kg balls at the sailors. When the Spanish ships are floating wrecks packed with battered and tired soldiers, the English will hop on board and finish them off.

5.4B Match of the day: England versus Spain

So what happened next?

King Philip's plan was an ambitious one. His fleet of 130 ships would sail up the English Channel to Calais and pick up Spanish soldiers waiting there for them. Then 30,000 soldiers and sailors would cross the Channel, capture London and capture Queen Elizabeth.

The Armada left Spain on 22 July 1588. But it was immediately spotted by a fast sailing boat heading for England. News that the Spanish were on their way would reach England long before they arrived – the English would know they were coming! Read the cartoon to find out the rest of this amazing invasion story.

1 130 ships set out, sailing packed together in a **crescent** shape, which the English would find difficult to attack.

2 The Spanish are spotted off Cornwall on 29 July and **beacons** are lit on hilltops to warn people of a possible invasion. The English Navy chases the Spaniards for over a week but cannot sink a single Spanish ship.

3 The Spanish arrive in Calais, France, on 6 August. They wait for Spanish soldiers to join them but the soldiers are delayed!

4 Sir Francis Drake attacks the Spanish ships with the weapon they fear the most – fireships. Eight old ships are filled with straw, gunpowder, tar, and barrels of pig fat and then set alight. They act like floating bombs and drift towards the Spanish, who panic when they see them.

5 Frightened by the fireships, the Spanish scatter in ones and twos, all over the North Sea. The fast English ships attack again and again.

6 The Spaniards flee. A sudden storm batters their ships as they struggle home around Scotland and Ireland.

7 Nearly every Spanish ship is damaged. The sailors starve as their food goes mouldy. Injured men die when their wounds become infected. As the ships sink, some sailors manage to stagger ashore, only to be attacked by the Scots and Irish.

SOURCE A: *The route taken by the Spanish Armada in 1588.*

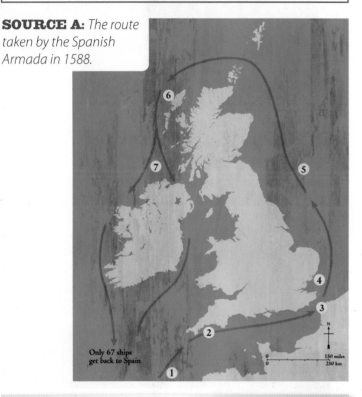

Only 67 ships get back to Spain

0   150 miles
0   250 km

'My health is not equal to this voyage. I know from my experiences at sea that I am always seasick and always catch a cold.'

▲ **SOURCE B:** *The commander of Spain's Armada was the Duke of Medina Sidonia. He was good at paperwork but had no experience of the sea or war, and he suffered from seasickness.*

The failure of the Spanish Armada proved that Spain was beatable. Spanish kings could no longer do as they wished. Elizabeth believed her island was safe from attack but would always need a strong navy to protect it. She began to build up a navy and soon it would begin to venture out in search of valuable new land all over the world.

Famous speeches

Some of the most famous lines in British history were spoken during the time of the Spanish Armada:

'I know I have the body of a weak and feeble woman, but I have the heart and stomach of a king, and a King of England too, and think foul scorn that… Spain… should dare invade the border of my realm.'

▲ **SOURCE C:** *This is part of the speech Queen Elizabeth gave to her troops on 18 August 1588. She was dressed in white and silver, and rode a white horse.*

Work

1 Sketch a map of the route taken by the Spanish Armada in 1588. Label your map with brief sentences, highlighting the most important events of the Armada's journey.

2 The following are all reasons why the Spanish Armada failed:
   · bad weather
   · fireships
   · faster English ships
   · the good leadership of the English
   · the delay of the Spanish soldiers at Calais.
   a Can you think of any others?
   b List the reasons for the Spanish failure. Start with the most important first.
   c Explain the reasons for your order.

3 Read the speech made by Queen Elizabeth I (**Source C**).
   a In your own words, paraphrase/explain what Queen Elizabeth was saying.
   b Why do you think we still remember those famous words today?

4 You have been asked to write a short feature on the Spanish Armada for a history magazine. Your feature will appear within the main article, which is called 'Famous naval battles'. Use the information on these pages to write an article of no more than 300 words.

Assessing Your Learning 2
Investigating Elizabeth's image

Queen Elizabeth was very keen to create an image of herself that would impress people. She wanted them to think she was powerful, rich, wise and beautiful. So she carefully controlled any pictures or paintings of herself so that she didn't look old, weak or ugly! She also made sure that any pictures of her were filled with symbols and special messages to show her power, her beauty, her achievements and her wealth. But can you spot them on this famous painting? Can you understand the messages and put all the clues together?

Imagine you work at Hatfield House in Hertfordshire. It is a large country mansion and the childhood home of Queen Elizabeth I. There are a number of objects on display connected to the queen, including a pair of her gloves. However, one of the most famous things on display is the portrait of Queen Elizabeth shown here. It is known as the Rainbow Portrait. Pretend you are about to talk to a group of students about the painting. You need to learn all about it and become a Rainbow Portrait expert – fast!

SOURCE A: *The Rainbow Portrait*

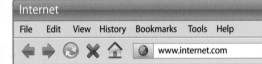

Internet

File   Edit   View   History   Bookmarks   Tools   Help

www.internet.com

Your task

You must write a short explanation or presentation (or even a speech) that outlines everything a visitor should know about the painting. When writing it, think about the student audience and the following:

- Include some basic background information on Queen Elizabeth herself. What have you learned about her from these pages and from other lessons in this book?
- When was the painting painted? And by whom?
- Describe the different symbols in the painting. What do they mean? What messages would they have given to people at the time?
- Why are paintings like this useful to us today? What do they tell us about Elizabeth and about Tudor times?

You will need to examine the painting in great detail and consult all the research sources here.

Who was Queen Elizabeth I?

- Born in 1533, the daughter of Henry VIII and Anne Boleyn.
- Queen of England, Ireland and Wales from 1558 to 1603.
- Her younger half-brother, Edward VI, and older half-sister, Mary I, ruled before her.
- She never married… but said she was married to her country instead!

Loading …

Rainbow Portrait

- Painted around 1600 by Isaac Oliver, a well-known portrait painter.
- Known as the Rainbow Portrait because of the rainbow Elizabeth holds in her right hand.
- She was well over 60 years old when this was painted... but looks much younger. Why was she painted to look so young?

Latin translation

Type Latin here:
Non sine sol iris

English translation:
No rainbow without the Sun

Notes:

What could 'no rainbow without the Sun' mean?

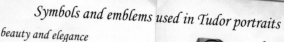
Symbols and emblems used in Tudor portraits

 beauty and elegance

 royalty

 pure/unmarried

youth

 fashionable in Tudor times, the large ruff looks like angel wings, perhaps trying to show she has been given her power by God or that God is with her

 she can see and hear everything so knows what is happening at all times

wisdom, intelligence, good judgement

hair down shows youth and long life

she brings peace after stormy times

good relationships between queen and advisers

There are several other very well-known portraits of Elizabeth (The Ditchley Portrait and the Armada Portrait, for example). Why not analyse them in the same way as this one?

Hungry for More?

Assessing your work

Look at the success criteria for this task to help you plan and evaluate your work.

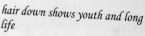
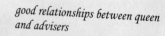

Good	In a **good** presentation, you would…	• outline several facts about Queen Elizabeth • select different symbols in the painting and explain what they mean • use clear and simple sentences and the correct dates and historical terms.
Better	In a **better** presentation, you would…	• outline why it was important for Queen Elizabeth to present her image in a certain way • select different symbols, explain what they mean and relate this information to the queen • produce clearly and carefully structured work, using the correct historical terms and dates.
Best	In the **best** presentation, you would…	• identify each symbol and explain its meaning • outline why a range of different symbols have been used in the painting • explain how paintings can be useful to historians • select, organize and use relevant information, using the correct historical terms to produce structured work.

In early 1603, Queen Elizabeth became seriously ill with pneumonia or bronchitis, both lung diseases. Despite this, she refused to rest properly and stood upright for 15 hours to show everyone that she was still strong. But soon she couldn't speak or eat and spent her days and nights lying on a pile of cushions staring at the fire.

Mission Objectives

- Explain why the throne of England passed to the Scottish royal family.
- Discover what England's new Scottish king believed about his 'Divine Right'.

Exit the Tudors

Despite being queen for 44 years, Elizabeth had never married or had any children. This worried her advisors. Who would rule after she died? Elizabeth had never said who she wanted to replace her. Perhaps she didn't want to think about dying! Now, in the queen's final days, her advisors named Elizabeth's third cousin, James VI of Scotland, as her successor. She nodded and raised her hand to show that she agreed.

Enter the Stuarts

In the early hours of the next morning, 24 March 1603, she died. A messenger called Robert Carey jumped on a fast horse and galloped up to Scotland to tell James. So James VI, King of Scotland, also became James I of England – one man with two countries to rule. Several weeks later, dirty, tired and injured after a fall on the way, the 36-year-old king arrived in London. The crowds that cheered him were witnessing one of the most famous changes of royal family in English history. The Tudor period had ended and now a new Scottish family, the Stuarts, had arrived to rule England.

FACT FILE: James I, 'the scruffy Stuart'

Name: James Stuart, the late Queen Elizabeth's third cousin.

Age: 36

Job title: King James I of England and King James VI of Scotland.

Early career: He was a successful King of Scotland. He managed to control rich and powerful lords and highland chiefs whenever they showed any sign of rebellion. He divided Scotland into districts and appointed royal judges to hold regular criminal trials. He invited weavers from abroad to teach Scottish clothmakers how to make better cloth that could be sold abroad, and encouraged gold, silver and coal mining. King James even managed to keep control of the Scottish (Protestant) Church!

Intelligence: A clever chap who wrote several books. His favourite subject was witchcraft. He also wrote about the dangers of smoking tobacco, which was a new fashion at the time.

Beliefs about being king: He believed that God had chosen him to be king – an idea called the **'Divine Right of Kings'**. As a result, he thought he could do no wrong. He wrote a book about this too!

Fashion: He wore padded clothes in case anyone tried to stab him. And if he got holes in an outfit he wouldn't change it, he'd just pull another item of clothing over the top!

Hygiene and manners: He never washed and he swore all the time. People also said that he picked his nose a lot and used his sleeve as a handkerchief when he had a cold.

Nicknames: None while he was alive but in 1625, Sir Anthony Weldon is said to have written, 'he was crafty and cunning in small things… but a fool in important matters'.

James and religion

When James I (VI of Scotland) arrived in England in 1603, he knew that one of his most important problems would be one that had troubled England's kings and queens for years – religion. As usual, people still quarrelled about religion (as they always had done), but clever Queen Elizabeth had worked hard to stop arguments between Catholics and Protestants.

However, when James met up with Church leaders in 1604, he failed to impress them. Some strict Protestants were so unhappy with the meeting that they left England forever. He also angered the Catholics when he ordered all their 'troublesome' priests to leave England. One small group of Catholics was so angry that they decided to launch one of the most famous murder plans in history – the Gunpowder Plot.

James and Parliament

The new king also managed to fall out with Parliament in a big way. James needed Parliament to help him rule – but didn't want them to argue with him about anything. When Parliament refused to collect money for the king, James sent all the politicians home… for ten years!

Instead, James asked his friends for help running the country – and found other ways to get money, like selling land and titles! However, despite managing to find ways to get lots of cash, James was even better at spending it – and by the time of his death in 1625, the king was nearly bankrupt.

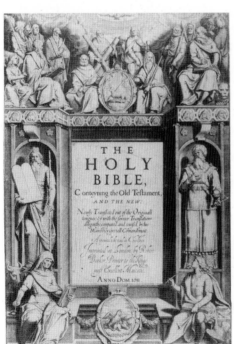

SOURCE B:

When James met with Church leaders at Hampton Court Palace in 1604, it was agreed that a new English translation of the Bible was needed. The King James Bible, as it became known, remained unchanged for 300 years and is the most printed book in history!

Divine Right of Kings

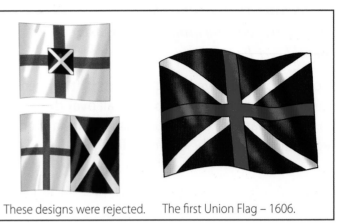

These designs were rejected.   The first Union Flag – 1606.

SOURCE A: *James quickly labelled himself King of Great Britain, although England and Scotland still ran their own affairs. In 1606, a competition was held to find a new flag that united both countries – the Union Flag.*

Work

1 On Queen Elizabeth's death, why was the King of Scotland asked to become King of England?

2 **a** Look at the fact file on James I, paying particular attention to the portrait. Write a description of James I's appearance, based on what you see.
   b Give a reason why this painting might not show the truth about James.
   c How does Sir Anthony Weldon describe James?
   d Sir Anthony had worked for James but was sacked by him in 1617. Does this make any difference to how we should treat his opinions?

3 **a** In your own words, explain what is meant by the 'Divine Right of Kings'.
   b Why do you think James was so keen on the Divine Right of Kings?
   c Can you think of reasons why Parliament might not agree with this idea?

4 Design your own flag to represent the union of England and Scotland under one king. Remember though – both the English and the Scots would have to like it.

5 Imagine you are a foreign ambassador who has just visited England (and met King James) in 1605. Write a short report about him to send home.

Remember, remember the fifth of November!

Remember, remember the fifth of November
Gunpowder, treason and plot.
I see no reason why gunpowder, treason,
Should ever be forgot...

Most of you will have heard this poem. It concerns an event so famous that millions of people all over the country still commemorate it – over 400 years after it happened. That legendary event is the Gunpowder Plot.

The Gunpowder Plot of 1605 has all the ingredients of a brilliant crime story. A plan to kill the king, gunpowder, betrayal, prison, torture, gun battles, hangings and fireworks. What a story!

Most of you will know the story quite well. Your friends and family will probably know the same tale. But do you know the full story? Was Guy Fawkes 'set up'? Did King James know about the assassination plot all along?

These two pages outline the familiar story of the Gunpowder Plot, the one you probably know already. The pages that follow (pages 88 and 89) then look at the evidence in detail. Then you will be challenged to make up your own mind. Were the gunpowder plotters framed? Firstly, though, let's look at the story most people are familiar with.

SOURCE A: *It is unlikely that the artist ever saw the plotters shown in this picture.*

King James I

In 1605, there were laws passed against people who were Catholic. King James had even ordered Catholic priests to leave England or face execution. A small group of Catholics decided that they wanted James dead. They hoped a new king or queen would treat them better.

The plot

Every year, the king or queen officially opened Parliament. In 1605, Parliament was due to be opened on 5 November and most of the powerful people in the country would go to watch. This ceremony still takes place today. The plot was to blow up the king when he was in Parliament, seize his young daughter, Elizabeth, and place her on the throne instead of James. Obviously, she would need help from older people, who would be Catholic, of course.

Plan A:
Early in 1604, Thomas Percy rented a house next to Parliament. The gang tried to tunnel under Parliament, just below where the king would sit. However, the tunnel soon filled with water.

Plan B:
In spring 1605, Percy rented a cellar directly under Parliament. Thirty-six barrels of gunpowder were smuggled in and stored behind piles of wood.

The plotters

Their leader was the brave and handsome Robert Catesby. He was a strict Catholic who had gambled away much of his family's wealth. He was joined by Tom and Robert Winter, the Wright brothers (Chris and John), Thomas Percy and of course Guy – or Guido – Fawkes. Guy was an experienced soldier who was used to handling explosives. He would be responsible for lighting the gunpowder to be placed under Parliament. There were many others who knew of the plan too.

What went wrong?

On 26 October 1605, a mysterious letter arrived at the house of a man called Lord Monteagle. The note contained a warning and Monteagle immediately took the note to Robert Cecil, who was the king's chief advisor. Cecil took the letter to the king.

'I would advise you… to devise some excuse to shift your attendance at the Parliament… they shall receive a terrible blow this Parliament and yet they shall not see who hurts them…'

▲ **SOURCE B:** *The mysterious letter contained this warning.*

By the early hours of 5 November, the cellars below Parliament were searched. A tall, brown-haired man was found hanging around. He was holding a lantern and had a watch, matches and a tinderbox in his pockets. He said his name was John Johnson and that he worked for Thomas Percy. He was brought before King James but refused to answer any of his questions. The king then ordered that he be taken to the Tower of London and questioned. After two days of torture on the rack he gave his real name as Guido Fawkes. After another two days he told his torturers that he was there to blow up Parliament. After another six days, he named the other plotters.

What about the others?

When the other plotters realized the plan hadn't worked, they barricaded themselves in Holbeche House, near Dudley, in the Midlands. They tried to dry out some of their wet gunpowder near a fire and, not surprisingly, it blew up. The noise from the explosion alerted the king's troops, who were searching nearby. After a shoot-out in which both Catesby and Percy were killed by the same bullet, the surviving plotters were arrested and taken to London. However, some would say Catesby and Percy were the lucky ones…

The punishment

After a quick trial, the survivors, including Guy Fawkes, were sentenced to death. They were dragged through the streets of London, hanged until they were nearly dead, cut down, cut open, and their insides were pulled out and burned on a fire in front of them. Then their corpses were cut into pieces and put on display around the country.

SOURCE C: *This picture shows the terrible punishments for the plotters.*

Guy Fawkes was probably dead before his punishment properly began. As he climbed up the scaffold steps with the hangman's noose around his neck, he jumped off head first and broke his neck. The execution carried on regardless.

Work

1 Explain what the plotters hoped to achieve by blowing up King James.

2 Write down the names of all the people connected to the story of the Gunpowder Plot. Next to each one, write down the role they played, for example, Lord Monteagle was sent the letter warning him of the plot to blow up Parliament.

3 a Read the passage taken from the unsigned letter to Lord Monteagle (**Source B**).
   b In your own words, explain the meaning of the letter.

4 Why do you think King James ordered such a nasty execution for the plotters?

5 🖊 **The Big Write!**

   📄 Imagine you were in London to witness the execution of Guy Fawkes and the remaining Catholic plotters. Write a letter to a friend describing the events of that day. Use **Source C** to help you. Remember, at the time most people were pleased that the plot had failed.

6 How do many people remember the Gunpowder Plot today?

6.3 Were the gunpowder plotters framed?

For hundreds of years, people believed the official government story of the Gunpowder Plot. Most people still believe this story today. It is the one that you read on pages 86 and 87. However, in recent years, some historians have found it difficult to accept this story. It has been argued that Robert Cecil, the king's minister and advisor, found out about the plot and even encouraged it. Cecil was a Protestant who wanted to make Catholics as unpopular as possible. What better way to do this than uncover a Catholic plot to kill the king?

Look carefully through the following evidence. Your task as a history detective is to hunt for clues, piece them together, and try to establish a clear picture of the plot to kill King James.

Robert Winter   Christopher Wright   John Wright   Thomas Percy   Bates

Evidence A

The 36 barrels of gunpowder were kept in a cellar next to Parliament. The cellar was rented to Thomas Percy by John Whynniard, a friend of Robert Cecil. Whynniard died suddenly and unexpectedly on the morning of 5 November.

Evidence B

All supplies of gunpowder were kept under guard in the Tower of London. The records for 1604 are missing.

Evidence C

Lord Monteagle took the warning letter to Robert Cecil on 26 October. The cellars below Parliament weren't searched until at least a week later.

Evidence E

Below are two examples of Guy Fawkes' signature whilst he was in the Tower of London. One was written just after his arrest; the other was scribbled a few days later. Why do you think the signatures are so different?

Evidence D

According to a Catholic visitor to London in 1604, Robert Cecil said:

'The king is too kind to Catholics. This gives great offence to others. We cannot hope for good government while we have a large number of people who obey foreign rulers as Catholics do. The Catholic priests preach that Catholics must even kill the king to help their religion.'

Evidence F

Below is part of Thomas Winter's confession, read out at the trial. He was one of the main plotters. The original confession has never been seen. A copy was written out by Robert Cecil for the trial.

'We were working under a little entry to the Parliament house. We under-propped it with wood. We bought the gunpowder and hid it in Mr Percy's house. We worked another two weeks against the stone wall, which was very hard to get through. At that time we called in Christopher Wright. About Easter we rented the cellar. After this Mr Fawkes laid into the cellar 1000 sticks and 500 bundles of firewood.'

Evidence G

One of the plotters, Francis Tresham, was Monteagle's brother-in-law. He was not caught straight away but was captured on 12 November. He died of a mysterious illness on 22 December, locked away in the Tower of London. Some said he'd been poisoned.

Evidence H

Holbeche House was surrounded on 7 November, only two days after Fawkes was captured. According to the government report, it took them two days of torture to get Fawkes to reveal his real name, let alone his part in the plot (another two days) and the names of the plotters (a further six days).

Guido
Fawkes

Robert
Catesby

Thomas
Winter

Be a Top Historian

Top historians will understand that we can **never really be sure** about certain events. The Gunpowder Plot is a good example of this. Some historians will say that the evidence proves that Robert Cecil knew about the plot all along. Others will say it proves we can't be sure. These disagreements are one of the things that make studying history so fascinating.

Work

 Now you have read all the evidence, it is time to put together your theory about the Gunpowder Plot.

Step 1 **Find evidence that the plotters were framed.**

Can you find any evidence of a connection between the plot and Robert Cecil? Did Cecil try to hide anything? Perhaps he even tried to stop people from talking? Do you think he knew details of the plot before it happened? Make notes on what you have discovered.

Step 2 **Find a motive.**

The king was not very popular at the time. Can you find any evidence to suggest why Cecil would 'set up' Catholic plotters and only catch them at the last minute? Write down your findings.

Step 3 **Think! Can we trust the evidence?**

Is there any reason not to trust the confessions of the plotters who were caught? Are they reliable? If not, why not? Write down the ideas that you have.

Step 4 **Time to wake up your mind, history detective! Were the plotters framed?**

Write a short paragraph outlining your theory. Was Cecil involved in setting up the plotters? Be sure to back up your ideas with some of the evidence.

People in Tudor and Stuart England were a very superstitious bunch. The day Queen Elizabeth was crowned, for example, was specially selected only after the stars had been studied for several weeks! Despite the fact that scientists were uncovering more and more about the world, people still didn't understand how animals could suddenly drop down dead or why a field of crops might fail one year. More often than not, when bad things happened in a town or village, it was concluded that a witch was at work. Witches, people thought, were the Devil's helpers, always on the lookout to do evil things and to help sinners find their way to hell!

Mission Objectives

- Explore why witchcraft was so widely believed in.
- Identify the type of people accused of witchcraft.
- Analyse sources from Stuart times.

The King's favourite subject

King James I was very interested in witchcraft and wrote a book suggesting different ways to catch witches. He wrote that all witches had strange marks on their bodies where they fed their 'familiars'. A '**familiar**' was a small creature – a toad or a cat, for example – that sucked on the witch's blood every night. The 'familiar', James wrote, was really the Devil himself in disguise! In fact, all sorts of 'witch-spotting' tips were published – they had no shadow, they talked to themselves, their hair couldn't be cut, they couldn't say the Lord's Prayer without making a mistake, and many more.

King James told Parliament to pass strict laws against anybody who was thought to be a witch and, in 1604, witchcraft became a crime punishable by hanging! Over the next 100 years, thousands of people were accused of witchcraft. The majority were poor old women – after all, they were the most likely to live alone with a pet and have strange marks on their body from a lifetime of hard work!

A witch trail

In James I's book, he claimed that the best way to identify a witch was to 'swim' them. This was a kind of trial. The accused would have their arms tied in front of them and a rope wrapped around their waist. They would then be thrown into a pond that would have been 'blessed' by a priest. It was thought that if the accused floated, they must be a witch because the 'pure' water didn't want them. They would be hanged. If they sank, the 'pure' water wanted them so they must be pure themselves and couldn't possibly be a witch – they were declared innocent (but dead!).

Witch-hunting

Witch-hunting was at its height in East Anglia during 14 terrible months between 1645 and 1646. An unsuccessful lawyer named Matthew Hopkins set up his own witch hunt, claiming that he had the Devil's list of witches. Hundreds of people were rounded up as a result of his enquiries – and most were women over the age of 50! He had 68 people put to death in Bury St Edmunds alone and 19 hanged in Chelmsford, Essex, in a single day. In fact, during these years, there were more cases of witchcraft in Essex courts than of any other crime, apart from theft. And after Essex, Hopkins set off for Norfolk and Suffolk where more people were accused!

SOURCE A: *This picture shows accusers 'swimming' a suspected witch.*

During the seventeenth century, about 2000 people were hanged as witches in England, Wales and Scotland before the 'witch craze' finally began to die down. Witchcraft ceased to be a crime in 1736. Britain's last victim, Janet Horne, was executed for witchcraft in 1727. Apparently, she had turned her missing daughter into a flying horse!

SOURCE B: *This print from a book of the time features Matthew Hopkins. He called himself the 'Witch Finder General' and he is pictured here surrounded by several 'familiars'.*

Wise Up Words

familiar

Work

1 Look at **Source A**.
   a In your own words, explain how the 'swimming test' was meant to identify a witch. Include details about the thinking behind the test.
   b Do you think this was a fair test? Write down the reasons for your answer.

2 Look at **Source B**.
   a Why has the artist drawn so many animals?
   b Write down five facts about the Witch Finder General.

3 Imagine the Witch Finder General himself is coming to your town and you want to impress him. Design a booklet that gives details about your town's efforts to catch witches. Include:
   • information about spotting a witch
   • successful convictions
   • drawings to show your witch trials.

4 Why do you think people in Tudor and Stuart times were so ready to believe in witchcraft and witches?

SOURCE C: *This German illustration, dated 1555, shows witches burning on a bonfire. Around 200,000 people were tortured, burned or hanged for witchcraft in Europe between 1500 and 1750!*

Why do Americans speak English?

Ever wondered why English is the most common language used in North America? After all, America is thousands of miles away from Britain, over the Atlantic Ocean – so why do most Americans speak English?

Mission Objectives

- Discover why and how the English began to settle in North America.
- Explain why most Americans speak English.

The story of the English language in North America starts in Tudor and Stuart times. Read the following cartoon strip carefully.

1 For thousands of years Native American (or American Indian) tribes lived in North America.

Great civilizations like the Aztecs and Incas could be found in Central and South America too.

2 In 1492 Christopher Columbus became the first recorded European to 'discover' the Americas. He was an Italian who was sponsored by Spain.

Other famous sailors followed Columbus but it was Spain and Portugal who began to dominate the world of exploration.

Hundreds of years before, Vikings had landed in Canada, so Columbus wasn't *really* the first!

3 By the mid-1500s, Spain controlled lots of land in and around the Americas, including Cuba, Panama, Jamaica, Chile, Ecuador, Peru and north-west Argentina.

Whilst Spain could boast of finding gold, tobacco, potatoes, tomatoes, cotton, sugar and rum in their new colonies, England had to be content with sailing to the northern part of North America… and finding cod! (They couldn't find any gold!)

4 With Spain controlling most of the trading routes to Central and South America, England's monarchs encouraged their sailors to concentrate on North America and try to find a route to the Spice Islands and India by sailing north of Russia and what we now call Canada.

Famous Englishmen like Sir Hugh Willoughby, Richard Chancellor, Sir Martin Frobisher and John Davis each got reputations as fantastic explorers and sailors.

5 In 1584, Queen Elizabeth gave permission to one of her favourites, Walter Raleigh, to start a settlement – or **colony** – in North America.

It was called Virginia after a name Elizabeth was known by – the Virgin Queen.

8 In September 1620, 102 men women and children tried yet again to start a new life in North America.

Thirty-five of the travellers were Puritans, unhappy with King James I, who would not accept their ideas about how God should be worshipped. A person who undertakes a religious journey is known as a **pilgrim** so the Puritans were sometimes called 'pilgrims'.

6 Over 100 settlers (or colonists) from England tried to start new lives in this new English colony but there was no good harbour, no easy way to make money and the local native tribesman often fought against the English.

When Raleigh tried to start a second colony in North America, all the new settlers found were the skeletons of the people from the first voyages. Later, the leader of the new settlers returned from Britain with supplies to find that all the settlers had mysteriously vanished!

7 In April 1607, a group of British settlers tried again to settle in America by moving to Virginia.

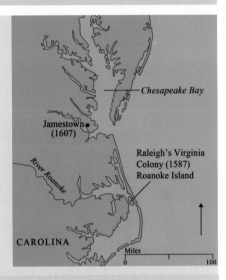

Chesapeake Bay

Jamestown (1607)

Raleigh's Virginia Colony (1587) Roanoke Island

River Roanoke

CAROLINA

Miles 0   100

They named their new settlement Jamestown in honour of King James I but they struggled to survive. By September 1607, half of the 104 colonists had died from disease and the local tribespeople remained hostile.

9 Their voyage in a small ship called the *Mayflower* lasted over two months. Food supplies went rotten and storms threw them off course.

Finally, they saw land on 9 December and started to build a small town where they came ashore. They named it Plymouth because they had set sail from Plymouth in England.

10 Life in their new home was hard. The settlers struggled to grow food – crops of wheat and peas failed. Fifty-one settlers died during the first winter from diseases such as pneumonia.

But the settlers were determined to survive and in the spring of 1621 they received help from an unexpected source.

11 A local native tribesman called Squanto showed the settlers how to plant 20 acres of corn and six acres of barley successfully.

He advised them how to fertilize the soil with dead fish! From then on the settlers knew how to farm successfully and life started to improve. Americans today are very proud of these hardworking settlers of 1620, who helped found their nation.

12 By 1624, over 120 people, including more settlers from Britain, were living in Plymouth, New England.

To celebrate their successful harvest – and to give thanks to God for their good fortune – the settlers tucked into a feast of turkey and goose. They invited the local tribesmen to join them.

13 This first meal enjoyed together by the tribesmen and settlers is still remembered in the United States of America today.

Every November, millions of American families have a day off work and sit down to a family meal of turkey, cranberry sauce and pumpkin pie. It is called Thanksgiving Day.

14 The success of the 1620 settlers encouraged others to leave Britain and move to the 'new world'.

They were joined by settlers from other countries, including France and Holland. In fact, Dutch settlers were responsible for building a town called New Amsterdam… later renamed New York!

15 Despite settlers from many other nations moving to the New World, it was the British who began to dominate the area and take over more and more land.

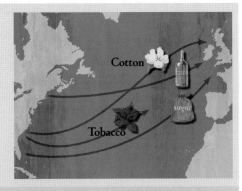

Soon, products grown in America, such as tobacco, cotton and sugar, began to flood into Britain, making some people on both sides of the Atlantic Ocean very rich.

16 By 1732, there were 13 British colonies in North America, remembered today by 13 stripes on the US flag.

It was now clear that British men, women and children – and the English language – were firmly rooted in North America.

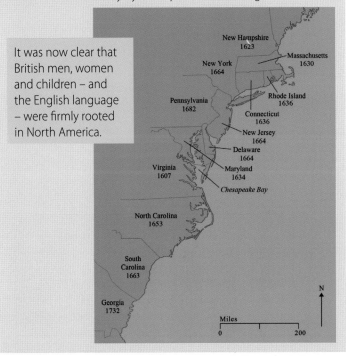

Wise Up Words

colony   Native American   pilgrim

Work

1 a Write a sentence or two about each of the following:
  - the Puritans
  - their reasons for leaving Britain
  - their journey on the *Mayflower*
  - the problems with their new home.

b Who helped the settlers with one of their problems?

c How did he help?

2 Look at **Source A**.

a List five foods, five items of clothing and five tools that settlers had to take with them.

b Why did some settlers not have to take as much as others?

c Why do you think the settlers had to bring so much equipment and food?

3 Imagine you are a settler who has briefly returned to Britain in 1620. People are constantly asking you what it is like in the New World. Prepare a speech to give to a group of Puritans who are unsure whether to take the trip. Try to convince them that travelling with you on your return journey is a good idea.

4 a How does Thanksgiving Day get its name?

b How did the pilgrims get their name?

Victual.
*Meal, one Hogshead.**
Beefe, one hundred waight.
Porke pickled, 100. or Bacon 74. pound.
Butter, two dozen.
Cheese, halfe a hundred.
Salt to save Fish, halfe a hogshead.

Apparell.
Shooes, six payre.
Boots for men, one payre.
Leather to mend shooes, foure pound.
Irish Stockings, foure payre.
Shirts, six.
*Handkerchiefes, twelve.**

Tooles which may also serve a family of foure or five persons.
One English spade.
One steele shovell.
Axes 3, one broad axe, and 2 felling axes.
One woodhooke.
One hammer.

For Building.
Lockes for Doores and Chests.
Hookes and twists for doores.

Find out what happened to Squanto. Why not try to write a mini biography?

Hungry for More?

◀ **SOURCE A:** *A list of things that a settler family was advised to take to America, printed in 1630. 'Victual' is food and drink. 'Apparell' is clothing. * means you could miss it out if you couldn't afford it.*

Why did the English start fighting each other?

In 1642, thousands of Englishmen went to war. They weren't going to fight the French, the Spanish or any other foreign country. They went to fight *other* Englishmen. England was at war with itself. We call this a **civil war**. So what made the English turn against each other? What were the long- and short-term causes of the conflict? And what were the two sides called?

Mission Objectives

- Examine why King Charles I, son of James I, had become so unpopular.
- Compare the two sides fighting the English Civil War.
- Define the term 'civil war'.

In most wars, there are two sides facing each other. The English Civil War was no different. On one side were King Charles I and his followers, known as the **Royalists**. On the other side were the men of Parliament and their followers. This group was known as the **Parliamentarians**. For many years, Parliament had worked with the king or queen. Now they were at war against the king. Parliament was meant to help make laws, discuss wars and raise taxes. However, first James I, and then his son Charles I, began to argue regularly with Parliament. They thought that Parliament was there to serve them… but Parliament thought differently. They thought that the monarch was there to serve his or her country! The argument would end in war. Look carefully at some of the key arguments taking place in the years building up to war.

King Charles I

I am the king and I can do as I like. This is my divine right because God has appointed me. Parliament thinks it can control its king by keeping me short of money. Parliament must be stopped… even if it means war.

Running the country is a difficult job and Parliament has been helping kings and queens for years. We like helping to make decisions but Charles only uses us to collect taxes for him. When we last refused to get him any more money, he sent us all home for 11 years and ruled without us. He only asked us back because a Scottish army invaded and he needed money to raise an army. The reason they invaded was Charles' fault too because he'd told the Scots to use a new prayer book they didn't like. Charles must change his ways… even if it means war.

William Cavendish, a rich lord

If Charles needs money, Parliament must get it for him. He is their king and God has put him on the throne. Parliament must allow a king to act like a king. But Parliament doesn't give Charles enough money and even ordered the execution of two of his personal advisors. Parliament must be stopped… even if it means war.

John Hampden, a Member of Parliament

There are more of us than ever before. We are strict Christians and our 'pure' way of worship is becoming popular. Many of us are Members of Parliament now. Charles has married a young Catholic princess. Is he trying to make the country more Catholic? We must stop him… even if it means war.

Harry Vane, a Puritan

I work very hard to make a good living. But Charles takes taxes from us without asking. His most recent idea was a charge for living by or near the sea. He calls it a **ship tax**. Charles must be stopped… even if it means war.

Laura Kibble, a farm worker

I will have to fight for Charles because my landlord told me to. He told me that Charles was appointed by God and I don't want to go against God's wishes. If Parliament is against Charles, they must be against God. They must be stopped… even if it means war.

Nicholas Farrall, a merchant

Wise Up Words

civil war   Parliamentarian   Royalist   ship tax

The two sides prepare for war

The final straw came when Parliament sent Charles a long list of complaints about him and his way of running the country. He was furious. He took 300 soldiers to London to arrest the five most troublesome Members of Parliament. However, when he got there, they had all escaped. Charles then left London and headed north to collect his army together. His queen went to the Netherlands to sell the crown jewels to pay for the war. Parliament started to bring its own army together. The English Civil War was about to begin.

Work

1   a   Explain what is meant by the following terms:
   - Royalist
   - Parliamentarian
   - divine right

   b   What is the main difference between an ordinary war and a civil war?

2   Copy the following statements into your book. Beside each, write either the word ROYALIST (if it would be the view of a supporter of the king) or PARLIAMENTARIAN (if this view would be held by a supporter of Parliament). Are any statements appropriate for both sides?
   - The king is chosen by God – he has a divine right to rule.
   - Parliament's job is to follow the king's commands.
   - No King of England should marry a foreign Catholic.
   - The king is there to serve his country – not the other way around!
   - One man cannot govern an entire nation.
   - This ship tax is unfair and illegal.

3   Could the Civil War have been avoided? What decisions could either side have made that would have stopped the war before it started?

4   Which side is mostly to blame for the Civil War – the king or Parliament? Give reasons for your answer.

On 22 August 1642, King Charles gathered his army together and stuck his Royal Standard (a big flag) into the ground in a field near Nottingham. It was the signal that the English Civil War had started. So what kind of people made up Charles' army? Who dared to fight against their king? And how did the two armies fight and work out who was on each side?

Mission Objectives

- Examine which sections of society supported each side in the Civil War.
- Summarize how soldiers fought in the Civil War and outline what they looked like.

Who was on each side?

Not too many people actually chose which side they were going to be on. They supported the side that got to their town or village first, or the side their local landowner supported. Friends would end up fighting friends, fathers might fight against their sons and so on. A woman might be married to a Parliamentarian but be sister to a Royalist! Civil wars were very nasty affairs. However, some groups of people knew exactly who they would fight for!

The rich lords and country gentlemen usually fought for the king. His support was strongest in the north of England, Wales, Devon, Cornwall and Somerset. Parliament was most popular in the south, especially London and other large towns and ports. Merchants, businessmen and Puritans would also fight for Parliament.

The Royalists were known as **Cavaliers**. 'Cavalier' comes from the Italian word *cavaliere*, which means soldier on horseback. The Cavaliers were known for their long hair and stylish clothes.

The Parliamentarians were nicknamed **Roundheads** because of their simple, short bowl-cut hairstyles.

The armies

The richer gentlemen on each side went into battle on horseback. The **cavalry**, as soldiers on horseback are known, wore steel breastplates over their leather coats. They tried to break through the enemy lines by firing their pistols and cutting men down with their swords.

Ordinary people on each side joined either the **pikemen** or the **musketeers**. Soldiers without horses were known as **infantry** or foot soldiers. As you couldn't easily tell who your enemy was by their appearance or language, both sides wore brightly coloured strips of cloth. The Royalists wore red **sashes** and the Parliamentarians wore yellow ones. That way, you could clearly see who was on each side.

The pikemen

These men were tough! The pikeman's job was to stand at the front of the whole army with a five-metre-long pole, a **pike**, tipped with steel. As the enemy approached, they dug one end into the ground and pointed the other at the charging enemy's horse. They wore heavy armour (who could blame them!) and also carried a sword.

The musketeers

A musket was a big clumsy gun. It was so heavy that musketeers (the men who fired them) needed a stick to rest it on! The gun was fired by using a 'match' (a piece of burning rope) to light the gunpowder that had been poured into the barrel. Hopefully, a ball or shot would fly out and travel up to 400 metres. It was a slow, complicated and very dangerous job – there was always a chance of accidentally blowing a finger off. One Royalist musketeer said, 'We seem to bury more fingers and thumbs than we do men.'

A musketeer and his musket – he would use his weapon as a club when the enemy got close

Lots of fighting

There were 635 different clashes between Cavaliers and Roundheads during the English Civil War. Sometimes the Cavaliers won, sometimes there was no clear winner and, on other occasions, the Roundheads claimed victory. One Royalist general and his troops even changed sides – but forgot to change their old red sashes to the new Roundhead yellow ones. They were all shot by their new **allies**.

A pikeman and his pike

Write a job description for either a musketeer or a pikeman, in order to try to recruit more men for your army. Try to include the following:
- Details of the job and responsibilities
- Equipment supplied
- Hazards of the job
- Benefits of the job.

Hungry for More?

Work

1 Who would usually:
   a   support the king?
   b   support Parliament?

2 Explain each of the following words:
   - Roundhead   • Cavalier   • cavalry
   - infantry   • musketeer   • pikeman   • ally

3 Look at the pictures of the pikeman and the musketeer. On which side did each fight? Explain how you made your choice.

4 a   Draw and label a picture of one of the types of soldier.
   b   Explain how your soldier would fight.

Prince Rupert: mad Cavalier or sad Cavalier?

Prince Rupert – nephew of King Charles I – was 22 years old when the Civil War began. He was a tall and handsome man who had been a soldier from the age of 13! He was put in charge of the Royalist cavalry and, apart from Charles himself, was the most famous Cavalier of the whole war. So what did he do to become so well known? And what did the Roundheads think of him?

Mission Objectives

- Recall who Prince Rupert was and why he was so popular with the king's supporters.
- Discover what the Roundheads thought of him and how they tried to damage his reputation.
- Define the word 'propaganda'.

The Royalists love Rupert

Rupert won fans because he was brave and fearless. He led brilliant cavalry charges and managed to capture several towns that supported Parliament. For example:

October 1642: He led the king's cavalry during battle of Edgehill. The battle was a draw.

June 1643: He stopped the Roundheads taking over Oxford.

July 1643: He captured Bristol.

May 1644: He captured other major ports.

June 1644: He saved York from Roundhead attack.

His best friend was his little white poodle called Boy. The dog went everywhere with Rupert, even into battle.

SOURCE A: *A portrait of Prince Rupert.*

Rupert was greatly admired by the Royalists and they lovingly nicknamed him the 'Mad Cavalier'. However, as you might expect, the Roundheads hated him.

The Roundheads hate Rupert

During battles, Roundheads looked carefully across the battlefield to spot him. It would have lifted their spirits to have killed Rupert… but no one seemed to be able to get near him. The Roundheads were also very **superstitious** about his dog, saying it was an evil spirit whose mother was a witch. Roundhead soldiers claimed that they had heard the dog talking (in several different languages) and that he had the power to make himself invisible. They thought that Boy's powers made his master unbeatable!

By the end of the year 1644, Rupert had avoided all attempts to kill him. Boy wasn't so lucky. He wandered onto the battlefield at Marston Moor in 1644 and was shot. Although the Roundheads never wounded Rupert in battle, they tried to wound him with words and pictures. This is known as **propaganda** and throughout history people have used it to say what they feel about other people. Things are written or drawn to give a one-sided message about someone. The writer or artist often makes things up too!

Look at **Sources B** to **E** very carefully. Each is about Prince Rupert or his dog. Think about the propaganda message that the writer or artist was trying to put across.

'They ran into every house cursing and damning, threatening and terrifying the poor women most terribly, setting naked swords and pistols to their breasts. They fell to *plundering* all the town, picking purses and pockets, searching in holes and corners and every other place they could suspect for money or goods... They beastly assaulted many women... and bragged about it afterwards, how many they had ravished... The next day in every street they kindled fire with gunpowder, matches, wisps of straw and burning coals.'

▲ **SOURCE B:** *This description of what Prince Rupert and his troops did in Birmingham in April 1643 was written by the wife of a Parliamentarian commander.*

▲ **SOURCE C:** *'The cruelties of the Cavaliers' was drawn by a man who supported Parliament.*

▲ **SOURCE D:** *This drawing by a Parliamentarian shows Rupert hiding in a field after defeat at Marston Moor in 1644. Look for: a) Roundheads capturing his baggage and wagons and discovering objects used by Catholics; b) his dead pet poodle, Boy. He is painted black to show he is dead.*

Wise Up Words

plundering   propaganda   superstitious

'Sad Cavaliers,
Rupert invites all you survivors
To his dog's funeral
Close mourners are the witch, Pope and devil,
Who regret the death of the late fallen evil.'

▲ **SOURCE E:** *This poem was taken from a leaflet printed to celebrate Boy's death.*

Be a Top Historian

Top historians should always be careful when looking at different sources. What a person writes, paints, or says is influenced by their own **attitudes and beliefs**. For example, a supporter of Parliament is highly likely to have a completely **different opinion** of King Charles from a Royalist!

Work

1   Why do you think Roundhead soldiers hated Prince Rupert so much?

2 **a** Explain what is meant by the word 'propaganda'.

   b Read **Source B**. How might this source be an example of propaganda?

   c What is the propaganda message in **Source C**?

   d Can historians be sure that the events in **Sources B** and **C** actually took place? Give reasons for your answer.

3   Read **Source E**. Do you think this poem was written by a Royalist or by a Parliamentarian? Give reasons for your answer.

4   Throughout the Civil War, the Roundheads tried hard to capture Prince Rupert. At one point they offered a reward for his capture... and his dog! Design a 'Wanted' poster for Prince Rupert and Boy. Try to include some examples of Roundhead propaganda in your design.

What was new about the New Model Army?

The first great battle of the Civil War – Edgehill in 1642 – ended in a draw… just! The commanders of Parliament's armies were shocked by the lack of discipline and skill shown by their troops. This was the first fighting that many of the soldiers had seen and they had been given very little training. In the chaos of battle, orders were ignored, soldiers fled in panic and it was impossible to control what the army was doing. The king's cavalry were experienced and well trained and very nearly wiped out Parliament's forces. So how did the Roundhead commanders react? What changes did they make to their forces? And what was it like to live and fight in the New Model Army?

Mission Objectives

- Summarize why Parliament needed to improve its army.
- Recall who was responsible for the training of Parliament's New Model Army.
- Examine how their strict discipline made them a more effective fighting force.

In order to improve their army, Parliament turned to a Member of Parliament from Cambridgeshire called Oliver Cromwell. They gave him the job of training a new set of troops to take on the king's men. This new fighting force was England's first truly professional army and, as it was a different kind of army, it was called the New Model Army. Cromwell made his troops live according to a strict code of conduct and harshly punished anyone who broke his rules. Read through the following sources carefully to discover what Cromwell's New Model Army was like.

'*These men were strictly trained and strictly disciplined. But above all, they fought for God. Singing hymns, they charged into battle and their discipline proved too much for Rupert's cavalry, for although the cavaliers were good horsemen, they were not always good soldiers.*'

▲ **SOURCE A:** *This view of the New Model Army is taken from a History textbook,* History Alive Book 1, *by Peter Moss (1980).*

'*Give me a russet-coated captain who knows what he fights for and loves what he knows, than that which you call a gentlemen and is nothing else.*'

▲ **SOURCE B:** *Cromwell said this in 1643. It shows that he chose his men based on their beliefs and values rather than their wealth. 'Russet' was the reddish-brown colour of the New Model Army's coats.*

'*Cromwell taught his cavalrymen to care for their horses and clean their weapons… regular drill [training] and strict discipline made his cavalry more manoeuvrable [easier to control] than the Royalist cavalry.*'

▲ **SOURCE C:** *This quotation is taken from* Oliver Cromwell and His World, *by Maurice Ashley (1972).*

Metal 'pot helmet'

Metal breastplate

Leather coat

Sword

Leather boots known as 'bucket tops'

Leather gloves

Lawes of the Army

Duties to God –
First let no man Blaspheme
[speak disrespectfully about] our
Christian Faith, upon paine to have his
tongue bored with a red-hot iron.

Duties towards Superiors and Commanders –
Resisting against correction – No man shall resist, draw, lift or
offer to draw, or lift his weapon against any officer.

Seditious [criticising Cromwell or Parliament] **words** –
None shall utter any words of sedition and uproar, or mutiny,
upon pain of death.

Moral duties –
Unnatural abuses – Any abusive or extremely violent behaviour,
shall be punished with death.
Theft – Theft and robbery, exceeding the value of twelve pence,
shall be punished with death.

Duties towards civilians [ordinary people not involved in the fighting] –
Waste and extortion – None in their Martch thorow [through] the countries
shall waste, spoile or extorte [take by force] any Victuals [food] or Money,
from any subject, upon pain of death.
Taking of Horses out of the Plow – No soldier shall take a horse out
of a plough, or wrong the Husbandmen [farmers], or cattel,
or Goods, upon pain of death.

Duties in camp and garrison –
Swerving from the camp – No man shall depart a mile out of the Army or
Camp without licence [permission], upon pain of death.
Offering violence to Victuallers – No man shall do violence to any that
brings Victuals to the camp, upon pain of death. Whosoever shall in
his quarter [the place where the soldiers lived], abuse, beat, fright his
landlord, or any person else in the family, shall be proceeded against
[treated] as a Mutineer, and an enemy to Discipline.

Duties in action –
Flying – No man shall abandon his colours, or flye away in Battail,
upon pain of death.
Flinging away arms – If a Pikeman throw away his pike, or a Musketeer
his musket, he or they shall be punished with death.

The secret of success

All that training and discipline paid off at the Battles of Marston Moor (1644) and Naseby (1645). Both were crushing victories for Parliament and, at Naseby, the king's army was all but destroyed by a series of complicated moves and brave attacks by Cromwell's men. On 5 May 1646, King Charles I realized he had no answer to Parliament's troops. He surrendered to Scotland, hoping he would be safe north of the border. But the Scots sold him to Parliament for a massive £400,000! Charles was brought to London for peace talks but soon escaped and fled to the Isle of Wight off the south coast. Soon, more fighting broke out (this is sometimes called the 'Second Civil War'), but it didn't last long. The king's troops were beaten and the king himself was arrested and brought to London (again). So what were Parliament going to do with him this time?

SOURCE D: *There was a tough code of discipline in the New Model Army. These are some examples of their 'lawes'.*

Work

1 a Why did Parliament need a New Model Army?
   b Who was given the job of training the men?
   c According to the sources, what sort of men did Cromwell want fighting for him?

2 Look at **Source D**.
   a This list was made public and pinned up around England. Why do you think Cromwell did this?
   b Why do you think the New Model Army rules were so strict?

3 Was the New Model Army a success? Give a detailed answer.

4 Pretend you are a captain in the army and you have been given the job of talking to a group of men who have just joined up to fight. Prepare a one-minute speech about the rules in Cromwell's New Model Army. Your opening line could be: 'Are you tough enough? You'd better be disciplined if you want to join us…'

Why was King Charles I sentenced to death?

King Charles and his Royalists lost the Civil War. England faced an uncertain future but nobody expected what happened next. At 2:00pm on 30 January 1649, King Charles had his head chopped off! But how did this happen? Why was he killed? And who sentenced him to death?

Mission Objectives

- Explore how and why King Charles was put on trial.
- Analyse the key events of the trial.
- Investigate how the judges arrived at their verdict.

By 1648 King Charles's troops had been beaten and he was being kept as a prisoner. In August the Scots invaded England on his orders. They were helped by those people who still supported Charles. The English Civil War was back on again.

However, the second Civil War didn't last long because the Royalist forces were easily beaten by Parliament's army. Many men in Parliament felt they couldn't trust the king any more and met to discuss what to do with him. Out of the 286 Members of Parliament, 240 thought Charles should be given another chance and reinstated as king. However, when they next met for discussion, those same 240 members were stopped from entering Parliament by Cromwell's troops. This left 46 Members of Parliament to vote about what to do with the king.

By 26 votes to 20, it was decided that Charles should be put on trial for treason. A jury of 135 top lawyers and judges were chosen to try him. The trial was fixed to start on Saturday 20 January 1649 in Westminster Hall, London. Now work your way through one of the most famous trials in history…

The trial

Day 1: Saturday 20 January 1649

Charles was brought to court by armed soldiers. A red velvet seat was brought for him to sit on. He refused to remove his hat but nobody forced him to. There were meant to be 135 judges but only 67 turned up.

'He is come, he is come and now we are doing the great work that the whole nation will be full of.'

▲ **SOURCE B:** *Oliver Cromwell said this after seeing King Charles walk to court on the first day of the trial.*

⚠ **STOP AND THINK**

How do Cromwell's actions compare to Charles'? Think about the actions of King Charles before the war started.

⚠ **STOP AND THINK**

Only 67 judges turned up on the first day. The wife of one man who didn't show up shouted out, 'He has too much wit to be here' when his name was read out. What do you think she meant?

SOURCE A: *A picture of the trial.*

First the charges were read out.

'Charles Stuart, King of England… traitorously waged a war against Parliament and the people. He renewed the war against Parliament in 1648. He is thus responsible for all the treasons, murders… burnings, damage and desolation caused during these wars. He is therefore a tyrant, traitor and murderer and an enemy to the commonwealth of England.'

▲ **SOURCE C:** *The crimes that Charles was charged with.*

⚠ **STOP AND THINK**
Read **Source C** very carefully. Make sure you have understood what the charges mean. You might need to look up words such as 'desolation', 'tyrant' and 'commonwealth'. In your own words, write a short paragraph describing the charges made against Charles.

The man leading the trial, John Bradshaw, asked Charles to say whether he pleaded innocent or guilty to these charges. Charles laughed and refused to plead at all. He said:

'I would know by what power I am called here. I want to know by what authority, I mean **lawful**. There are many unlawful authorities in the world, thieves and robbers on the highway… Remember, I am your king, your **lawful** king… I have a trust committed to me by God, by old and lawful descent; I will not betray it to answer a new unlawful authority.'

▲ **SOURCE D:** *The king's response to the charges.*

⚠ **STOP AND THINK**
Why do you think Charles uses the word 'lawful' so often? What do you think 'I have a trust committed to me by God' means? Throughout the trial, Charles refused to take his hat off, interrupted and even laughed at what was being said. Why do you think he behaved like this?

The day ended with Charles refusing to plead innocent or guilty – he even refused to accept that the court had any legal right to put him on trial.

Wise Up Words

commonwealth   death warrant   desolation
execution   revolution   tyrant

Day 2: Monday 22 January 1649
Seventy judges turned up on the second day. The court continued to ask Charles to plead innocent or guilty to the charges. Charles argued that the courts were the king's courts and under his authority – so how could the king be put on trial in his own court? At one point, Charles and Bradshaw appeared to argue with each other (see **Source E**).

Bradshaw: *Confess or deny the charge.*

King: *By what authority do you sit?*

Bradshaw: *We sit here by the authority of the Parliament of England and you are responsible to them.*

King: *I deny that! Show me one precedent.*

Bradshaw: *This is not to be debated by you.*

King: *The Parliament of England is not a Court of Law.*

Bradshaw: *It is not for prisoners to discuss.*

King: *Sir, I am not an ordinary prisoner.*

Bradshaw: *Take him away.*

▲ **SOURCE E:** *The king and Bradshaw argued. 'Precedent' means where something has happened before. Why did Bradshaw become so frustrated with Charles?*

Work

✏ **The Big Write!**

It is 1649 and you have managed to get a seat in the gallery to watch the trial of Charles I. Write a short letter to a friend about the events of days 1 and 2. Remember to follow the conventions of a letter, including your address, your friend's address and the date.

IMPORTANT: Choose whether you are either a supporter of Charles OR a supporter of Parliament. Your letter should reflect your feelings. For example, a supporter of Charles might think his refusal to take his hat off was brave and courageous. Someone against him might think this was disrespectful to the judges.

Why was King Charles I sentenced to death?

The trial continues...

Days 1 and 2 of King Charles's trial did not go well. Some of the judges didn't turn up and the king still refused to plead guilty or not guilty. So what happened next?

Day 3: Tuesday 23 January 1649

Seventy-one judges turned up on the third day. Once again, Charles refused to plead. He said that the court, which was chosen by the army, relied on force, not the law. He added, 'How I came here I know not, there is no law to make your king your prisoner.' Charles was taken away again after just a few minutes in court.

Look at the first three days of the trial. In your opinion, is the trial going better for the king or his enemies?

Days 4–6: 24–26 January 1649

Things weren't going as Parliament and Cromwell had hoped. Algernon Sidney, a leading judge, who refused to take part in the trial, said publicly, 'Firstly, the king cannot be tried by any court and secondly, no man should be tried in this court.'

The judges met without Charles for the next few days. They decided to write down a plea of 'guilty' despite the fact that Charles had chosen not to answer any of their questions properly. Finally, witnesses were heard.

Witness No. 1:
'I saw Charles stick his banner in the ground in Nottingham in 1642. This officially started the war. The war was Charles' fault.'

Witness No. 2:
'King Charles once saw some of Parliament's troops being badly treated by Royalists. He said, "I do not care if they cut them three times more, for they are my enemies."'

Later that day, the judges made their decision. They decided that Charles was guilty of all charges and called him to see them the next day.

Verdict and Sentence
Day 7: Saturday 27 January 1649

Sixty-eight judges were there on the final day. Charles entered the hall (with his hat on) and sat on his chair. Bradshaw said that it was the duty of any king to talk with Parliament frequently. Charles hadn't done this and so had failed in his duties as a king. This started the war. At this point, Charles tried to make a statement but wasn't allowed to do so. Then Bradshaw pronounced the king 'guilty' and read out the sentence (see **Source A**).

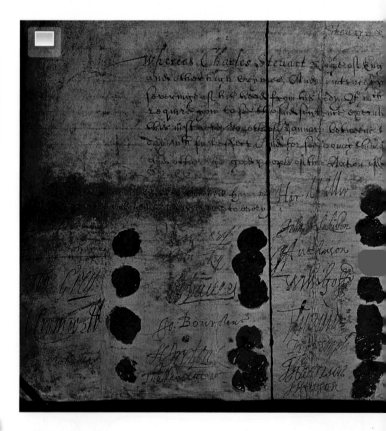

Witness No. 3:
'Here is a letter from King Charles to his son. He is asking his son to get a foreign army together to invade England. Charles wants foreigners to kill Englishmen. He can't be trusted... he's a traitor.'

'This court does judge that Charles Stuart, as a tyrant, traitor, murderer and a public enemy, shall be put to death by the severing of his head from his body.'

▲ **SOURCE A:** *The death sentence passed on King Charles.*

The **execution** date was set for Tuesday 30 January 1649. The **death warrant** (a signed piece of paper that confirms that a person will be executed) was signed by 59 judges… who then went off to pray!

'I tell you, we will cut off his head with the crown upon it.'

▲ **SOURCE B:** *Oliver Cromwell speaking in January 1649.*

SOURCE C: *Charles I's death warrant. Forty men signed it straight away but others had to be forced to sign it.*

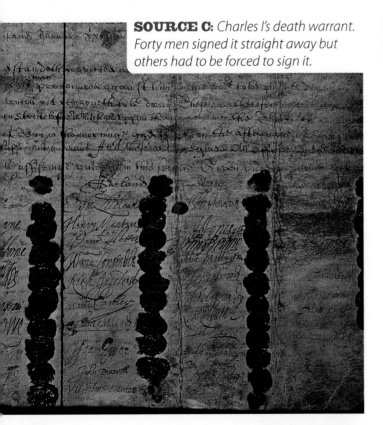

SOURCE D: *Bradshaw wore this metal-lined hat during the trial. Why do you think he did this?*

Be a Top Historian

Top historians should understand that an event, such as the execution of King Charles, could have many **consequences**, and that these consequences can be both **short-term** and **long-term**. Make sure you know what short-term and long-term consequences are.

Work

1 Look carefully at the death warrant in **Source C**. Can you make out any of the names? Look for Oliver Cromwell's signature.

2 Look at **Source B**. Write a sentence or two describing Cromwell's attitude to the trial.

3 Only 59 judges signed the death warrant. Look again at page 104 and find out how many people were first chosen to make up the jury. What does this tell you?

4 Look up the word 'revolution' in a dictionary. Is this a suitable word to describe the events of 20–27 January 1649?

5 🖊 **The Big Write!**

📄 Write another letter to your friend (or continue with your letter from the previous page), about the events of days 3–7. This time you will have to include your opinion of the verdict. Remember, you are writing as a supporter either of Parliament or of Charles. Make sure you follow the conventions of a letter, including your address, your friend's address, and the date.

Hungry for More?

Why not write a short script for, and perform, a role-play about the trial of King Charles? In groups, take on the roles of Charles, Bradshaw, the spectators and the judges. You will also need a narrator to tell the story of the trial.

We all know that there weren't any televisions at the time of King Charles' execution. There were no six o'clock news programmes, no newsflashes and certainly no special live reports. However, if there were, the events of Tuesday 30 January 1649 might have been presented like this…

Mission Objectives

- Explore how Charles spent the last few hours of his life.
- Examine the details of his execution.
- Evaluate sources relating to the execution.

TV presenter: We are very sorry to interrupt your Tuesday afternoon film but the news we have been expecting has just been confirmed. Charles Stuart, King of England, is dead. Shortly after 2:00pm, he was beheaded outside Whitehall Banqueting House, London. Over to Annette Ball, our live reporter at the scene.

Live reporter: Thank you, Linda. We are witnessing amazing scenes here in London today. The execution was planned for around 12 noon, so early this morning the king went for a walk through St James' Park with his pet spaniel, Rogue. He ate some bread, drank some red wine and then insisted on putting on two shirts before he started his final journey.

TV presenter: Why two shirts, Annette?

Live reporter: It's very chilly here today in London, Linda, and apparently Charles didn't want to start shivering from the cold. He didn't want the public to think that he was trembling with fear.

TV presenter: You say that they planned to execute him at 12 noon but he was killed shortly after 2:00pm. Why the delay?

Live reporter: Firstly, the usual executioner refused to do it. Then 38 other men were each offered £100 to do it. One by one they refused. Eventually, two men agreed to do it in disguise. They wore masks, wigs and false beards.

TV presenter: So what happened next?

Live reporter: The king arrived shortly before 2:00pm. He stepped out onto the black cloth-covered scaffold, took off his jewels and his cloak, and then tucked his hair into a cap. He spoke calmly to those men near to him, kneeled down to pray and then put his head on the block.

TV presenter: Was it a clean cut, Annette?

Live reporter: Yes it was, Linda. One clean chop. Then one of the axemen held up Charles' head for all to see. An eyewitness told me, 'There was such a groan by the thousands then present, as I never heard before and desire I may never hear again.'

TV presenter: Describe the scene now, Annette.

Live reporter: The king has just been taken away in a wooden coffin. Now people are paying to dip their handkerchiefs in the king's blood. Others are trying to break off pieces of the scaffold covered in his blood. Some of the soldiers guarding the scaffold will make a fortune today! Incredible scenes, Linda. What can the country expect next? Back to you in the studio…'

TV presenter: That's the big question tonight. King Charles is dead… so what happens now? What will Parliament do?

And that must have been the question on everyone's lips. With no king, what sort of job would Parliament do?

Wise Up Words

bias

SOURCE A: *This woodcut of the execution, was created straight after the event.*

SOURCE B: *This painting of the execution was painted soon after the event.*

Work

1 a Why do you think so many people refused to execute Charles? Give as many reasons as you can.

b Why did the two men finally agree to do it?

c Think carefully. Why did the executioners insist that Charles tuck his long hair into a cap?

2 Look at **Source A**. What is wrong with this print? Your answer to **1b** might give you a clue.

3 a Look at **Source B**. You will notice four smaller pictures surrounding the main one. Describe what you think each of the smaller pictures shows.

b Why do you think that a woman in the main picture has fainted?

c Why do you think some people wanted to dip their handkerchiefs in the dead king's blood?

4 **The Big Write!**

Design the front page for a broadsheet newspaper in 1649 reporting the amazing events of Charles' execution. Try to do the following:

- Write a version that favours either the supporters of the king or those who decided to execute him.
- Show your report to a classmate and see if they can spot the parts of your writing that show **bias**.

The man who banned Christmas

When King Charles I was executed in January 1649, the country became what's known as a **republic**. This is the name given to a country without a king or queen. Things would stay like this for the next 11 years. So what was life like in the republic? If there wasn't a king or queen, then who made all the laws and decisions? And why was the decision made to ban Christmas?

Who rules?

Without a king or queen, people looked towards the most powerful man in the country to guide them. That person was Oliver Cromwell, the leader of the army that had beaten King Charles' men (see **Source A**).

Who was Cromwell?

Cromwell was a Member of Parliament and a brilliant army leader. He was also a Puritan. Puritans were strict Christians who read the Bible closely as they believed it taught them how to live their lives. They tried to lead simple lives like Jesus, wear plain clothes and eat ordinary food. They didn't like sports and entertainment because they thought these distracted people from worshipping God. By the 1650s, there were lots and lots of Puritans in the country, including Oliver Cromwell.

SOURCE A: *In this painting, Oliver Cromwell is looking at the body of King Charles I. The artist is well known for painting famous historical events that he did not witness and may have been only legends, so this scene may not have actually happened.*

Parliament rules... or does it?

To start with, Parliament ruled the country but soon the politicians began to argue amongst themselves. So Cromwell, who was greatly respected by many, closed Parliament and decided to run the country himself. He was called **Lord Protector** and paid a huge salary of £100,000 a year. Cromwell divided the country up into 11 districts and appointed a **Major-General** to run each one. These men were strict Puritans and introduced many new laws. **Source B** shows some of the things that were banned.

BANNED! By order of the Major General (because pleasure and enjoyment are wicked)

Football banned

Inns shut

Bear-baiting stopped

Theatres closed

Maypole dancing stopped

Gambling banned

▲ **SOURCE B:** *Puritan rule was very strict and laws like the ones above made the Puritan rulers increasingly unpopular.*

What about Christmas?

A proposed law in 1650 tried to stop women wearing make-up and swearing was outlawed. In 1656, a woman was fined 12 shillings (60 pence) for saying seven rude words. And there were no more feast days, such as May Day or All Saints' Day, either. Instead, a fast day was introduced once a month, and eating and drinking was completely banned on Christmas Day – no ale, no mince pies, no pudding! In 1652, soldiers even went around houses at Christmas dinnertime to take away any meat.

Fed up!

By 1658, Cromwell and the Major-Generals were becoming very unpopular. Many ordinary people didn't want to live by these strict laws any more. Lucy Hutchinson, who was once one of Cromwell's strongest supporters, wrote: ' the whole land grew weary of him, while he set up a company of silly, mean fellows, called Major-Generals'. In September that year, Oliver Cromwell died. So what would happen to the country next?

SOURCE C: *Puritans led simple lives, wearing plain clothes (usually in black and white) rather than bright, fashionable ones. They wanted simple churches too – plain glass replaced stained glass, church bells were removed, candlesticks were melted down and organs smashed up.*

FACT!

Cromwell himself wasn't a particularly strict Puritan. He drank alcohol, played bowls and liked music and hunting.

Work

1 a Write a sentence to explain the following words:
 • republic   • Interregnum

 b What was the difference between the Lord Protector and a Major-General?

 c Why do you think Cromwell gave himself the title of Lord Protector?

 d Why do you think the Major-Generals were so unpopular with some people?

2 Write a paragraph explaining how a) churches and b) entertainment changed during the Interregnum.

3 Produce a 'warning' poster for Cromwell's England. Imagine that it would be displayed at the time. It should warn people what they are not allowed to do… and why. Use no more than 25 words on your poster.

Cromwell: curse of Ireland?

There are no statues of Cromwell in Ireland. In fact, when the Irish Prime Minister visited an important British politician in the 1990s, he marched straight back out of his host's office as soon as he arrived. When asked why he had left, the Irishman said, 'I'm not coming in until you take down the picture of that murdering *@*#*&*'! He was talking about the portrait of Oliver Cromwell that was hanging over the mantlepiece. So what did Cromwell do to become so hated in Ireland? And does he deserve his terrible reputation there?

Mission Objectives

- Recall how Cromwell is viewed in Ireland.
- Analyse what he did to earn his reputation in Ireland.
- Judge whether he deserves his terrible reputation.

England and Ireland

English rulers had been interfering in what was going on in Ireland since the 1100s. Many English kings had tried to rule Ireland and Henry VIII even called himself the King of Ireland, without ever even visiting!

Some Tudor monarchs thought they would have a better chance of controlling Ireland if they sent English people to live there. As you can imagine, the Irish weren't very happy with foreigners turning up and taking their best land.

By 1640, over 25,000 Englishmen (and many Scots) had gone to live in Ireland. The **settlers** were Protestant while the Irish remained Catholic. In 1641, the hatred between the two groups burst out into violence and the Irish killed thousands of English and Scottish settlers. The English wanted revenge, but for a while they were distracted by the English Civil War and were unable to sort things out.

Cromwell and Ireland

Irish Catholics supported Charles I during the English Civil War (Charles was married to a Catholic, after all). When Charles lost his head, the Irish still supported his son, the future Charles II. England's new leader, Oliver Cromwell, decided to deal with the Irish once and for all and took an army of 12,000 men with him, landing in Ireland in August 1649. He laid **siege** to the town of Drogheda and demanded that the Irish army inside surrender. He said he would attack if they didn't.

What happened next earned Cromwell a nickname. Even today, Cromwell is known to many as the 'curse of Ireland'. These pages examine why and ask if he deserves the nickname. Read through the sources carefully.

'So that spilling of blood may be prevented, I thought it right to summon you to surrender this place. If this is refused, you will have no cause to blame me.'

▲ **SOURCE A:** *Letter written by Cromwell to Sir Arthur Aston, who commanded the Royalist soldiers in Drogheda.*

'I forbade them to spare any people in the town who had weapons, and I think that night they put to sword about 2000 men... About one hundred fled and entered Saint Peter's church steeple, some the west gate and others a strong round tower next to the gate called Saint Sunday's. These being asked to yield in the name of mercy, refused, whereupon I ordered the steeple of Saint Peter's church to be set on fire.'

▲ **SOURCE B:** *Part of Cromwell's report to Parliament about the siege of Drogheda. The word 'yield' means surrender.*

'The soldiers threw down their weapons on an offer of quarter. The enemy entered Mill Mount without resistance. They put every soldier to the sword and all the citizens who were Irish, man, woman or child.'

▲ **SOURCE C:** *Written between 1668 and 1670 by the Duke of Clarendon, a Royalist. He was in France at the time of the attack.*

An offer of quarter was an opportunity to surrender. The rules of war at the time meant that if an enemy was given the chance to surrender, and didn't take it, they could be killed later if they were caught. But if they did surrender, it would be wrong to kill them.

'The Royalists fled over the bridge where some of them were killed. Some got into two towers of the wall and some into the steeple of a church. The steeple was set on fire and then fifty of them got out at the top of the church but our angry soldiers put them all to the sword and thirty were burned in the fire. Those in the towers were given mercy. In this slaughter there were at least 3000 dead bodies in the fort and streets.'

▲ **SOURCE D:** *Letter written by one of Cromwell's soldiers in October 1649.*

Each of the attackers [Cromwell's men] picked up a child and used it as a shield to keep themselves from being shot. After they had killed all in the church, they went into the vaults underneath where all the women had hid themselves.'

▲ **SOURCE E:** *Written by Thomas Wood, an eyewitness. It appeared in 1663, five years after Cromwell's death. Charles II was then king, and he hated Cromwell.*

'At the garrison of Drogheda, about 3000 men and priests, women and children were slaughtered without mercy… At Wexford garrison 2000 men and civilians were also butchered. [In Ireland] Catholic worship was banned. More than a third of the Irish land was confiscated… Irish landowners were forced to move to western Ireland.'

▲ **SOURCE F:** *From a modern history book,* The World of Enlightenment *by Bea Stimpson (1999).*

'As a result of those killed in the wars, those sold as slaves and those who fled abroad, the population of Ireland was reduced by half, and there were sown the seeds of hatred towards the English that have lasted in some places until the present day.'

▲ **SOURCE G:** *From a modern history book,* History Alive Book 1 *by Peter Moss (1980).*

SOURCE H: *This illustration shows the siege of Drogheda in 1649.*

Work

Does Cromwell deserve the title of the 'curse of Ireland'?

1   Which evidence supports the theory that he simply followed the rules of war and gave the Irish the chance to surrender? Does any evidence suggest that no option of surrender was given? Can we trust all the evidence to be true? Make notes on your findings.

2   What acts of violence took place at Drogheda? How many people do you think were killed there? Were women and children killed? Can we trust all the evidence? If not, why not? Write down your findings.

3   What effect did Cromwell's actions have on Ireland? Was the population of Ireland affected in any other way? Did Cromwell's actions shape many Irish people's attitudes towards the English and Cromwell in particular? Make notes on your findings.

4   Now present your ideas. Write a paragraph outlining your opinions of Cromwell's actions at Drogheda and afterwards. Was he truly the 'curse of Ireland' or simply a soldier doing his duty according to the rules of war?

Oliver Cromwell is one of the most famous men in British history. Apart from Queen Victoria, more streets in Britain are named after him than anyone else. And more books have been written about him than about any king or queen. But what makes Cromwell so well known is the fact that he divides opinion. To some he was a great man who changed the way Britain was run and made it a safer and fairer place to live. But to others he was a power-hungry monster who made Britain a worse place to live while he was Lord Protector. So what do you think?

Mission Objectives

- Examine why people admired and respected Cromwell.
- Examine why others disliked him.
- Judge whether you think Cromwell was a hero or a villain.

SOURCE A: *This statue of Cromwell stands outside the House of Commons in Westminster, London.*

Look through the following pieces of information and opinions about Oliver Cromwell's time as leader of the country. Think about whether they support the view that Cromwell was a hero or a villain. Or do some support the view that he was a hero *and* a villain?

A

Cromwell rose to become a brilliant soldier and a respected politician. And he promoted people based on their abilities, not on who their parents were or how much money they had.

B

Cromwell always said that it was better for the country that King Charles I was executed because he couldn't be trusted and wasn't prepared to work with Parliament.

C

Under Cromwell, the army improved and was both feared and respected by France and Spain, which made the country safer and stronger.

During Cromwell's reign, theatres were closed and music, gambling and dancing were banned. Boys caught playing football on a Sunday were whipped!

D

E Cromwell himself enjoyed music, hunting and playing some sports. At his daughter's wedding, there was dancing and violins were played.

F Cromwell ended a war with the Netherlands and ceased hostilities with Portugal. He controlled Scotland, Ireland and Wales too.

G Cromwell sometimes put his enemies in prison and acted without the consent of Parliament. He was against the idea of allowing all the people to vote.

In Ireland, Cromwell slaughtered people who refused to surrender to him. This included men, women and children. Thousands of Irish children were sent to be slaves in the West Indies.

H

J

Cromwell wanted Parliament to rule the country. But when the politicians tried to restrict people's freedom to worship how they wished, Cromwell said that was wrong and dismissed Parliament.

I In 1290, all Jews were expelled from the country. Cromwell allowed Jews to come back into the country and worship how they wanted to.

K Without Parliament, Cromwell ruled on his own — a bit like a king! The country was divided into 11 areas, each with its own Major-General, who set taxes and made laws. They were very unpopular.

Work

1 **a** Makes a list of opinions that support the idea that Cromwell was a hero.

   b Make another list of opinions that support the idea that he was a villain.

   c Have you struggled to place some in one of the categories? If so, explain why.

2 In your opinion, was Cromwell a hero or a villain… or both? Explain your view.

3 In museums, exhibits often have short explanations about what they show, called captions. Imagine you've been asked to write a museum caption on Cromwell for a newly discovered portrait of him. Try to sum up what sort of person Oliver Cromwell was in no more than 100 words.

Whatever happened to Cromwell's head?

Oliver Cromwell died of **malaria** in September 1658. His funeral cost around £50,000 and was the biggest ever seen. Around 30,000 soldiers escorted his coffin to Westminster Abbey, London, where it was buried. But it didn't stay there long! A few years later Cromwell's body was dug up… and his head was cut off. These pages examine why this happened – and what happened to his head over the next 300 years.

Cromwell Junior

After Oliver Cromwell's death, his son Richard was made Lord Protector. But he didn't really want the job and would rather have been left alone to work on his farm. Unable to stop the arguing between Parliament and the army, Richard resigned after only a few months.

Charles returns

After a few more months of confusion, a new Parliament asked Charles I's son (also called Charles) to return to the country from abroad to become king. So in 1660, the nation had a monarchy again. And one of the new King Charles II's first actions was a brutal one. He decided to kill the men who had killed his father!

SOURCE A: *Cromwell and Bradshaw were 'executed' in 1661. Henry Ireton, who was also already dead, was 'executed' with them. He had also signed the death warrant, was a key soldier in Cromwell's army and was also his son-in-law.*

Hunting the 'king killers'

Fifty-nine people had signed the death warrant for King Charles I in 1649. Fifteen of them were already dead by 1660, including Oliver Cromwell and the main judge, John Bradshaw. The new king ordered that the bodies of the leaders should be taken out of their coffins and publicly hanged at Tyburn (near Marble Arch in London today). Afterwards, their heads were cut off and stuck on spikes outside the building where Charles I's trial had taken place. Their bodies were thrown into a pit.

But Charles II didn't stop there. Whilst some of the men who had signed his father's death warrant had escaped abroad to America and Switzerland, many others were still in Britain and were arrested. Several died in prison, but 13 of the **regicides** (the correct name for a person who kills a monarch) were executed. (See **Source A**.)

So what about Cromwell's head?

The story of Oliver Cromwell's head, which was stuck on a spike outside Westminster Hall in London, is fascinating – and disgusting. Look through the cartoon strip carefully.

Wise Up Words

malaria   regicide

1658: Cromwell dies. Doctors examine his body and decide to weigh his brain. They say it weighs 82.5 ounces. The average brain weights 49 ounces… so they were probably lying! Can you think of any reasons why the doctors might have said Cromwell had a bigger brain than he really did?

1660: King Charles II becomes king and wants to punish Cromwell, who is already dead! So Charles orders Cromwell's body to be removed from Westminster Abbey and hanged at Tyburn. Cromwell's head is then stuck on a 6-metre pole nearby.

1685: Cromwell's head stays on the pole for over 20 years but is eventually blown off in a storm. A soldier named Barnes finds it and takes it home. A reward is offered for the return of the missing head, so Barnes, who was warned he might get in trouble for taking it in the first place, hides it in a chimney.

1702: As Barnes lies dying, he tells his family where he's hidden the famous missing head. The head is found and eventually ends up in the possession of a French-Swiss man called Claudius Du Puy, who puts it in a museum in London.

1738: The museum owner dies and an actor called Samuel Russell buys it from Du Puy's relatives. He pays his rent by charging people to see it.

1787: When Russell gets into debt, he is forced to sell the head. A group of businessmen eventually buy it for £230 (over £7000 in today's money). They hope eventually to charge people to see it and put it on display in Bond Street, London.

1814: By now, the displayed head isn't making the owners much money, so it is sold to a man named Josiah Wilkinson. He keeps it in a box, wrapped in silk. Wilkinson writes that there is an ear missing, a hole in the top of the head where a spike has been, and axe marks on the neck.

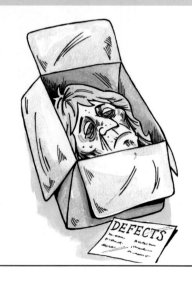

1935: A descendant of Wilkinson allows the head to be examined by experts. A 109-page report is written, stating that the head had definitely been chopped off and that the pimples and warts match portraits of Cromwell. It is concluded that the head is indeed Oliver Cromwell's.

1960: Wilkinson's descendant decides the head should be buried properly. It is given to Cromwell's old college in Cambridge where it is buried secretly. It is still there today.

SOURCE A: *This portrait of Oliver Cromwell was painted in 1656. He told the artist, 'Do not flatter me at all, but show all the wrinkles, pimples and warts.'*

FACT!

Historians are confident that they know the story of Cromwell's head, but mystery still surrounds what happened to the rest of Cromwell's body! Experts think that it was probably thrown in an unmarked grave near Tyburn. In the 1980s, builders found several skeletons without skulls buried near where Cromwell's body was supposedly buried… but no one could be sure if one of them belonged to him!

Be a Top Historian

Top historians are often asked to judge how **significant** an event or an individual has been. To be 'significant', an individual or event must have changed people's lives, often in many ways. So, would you regard Oliver Cromwell as a significant person?

SOURCE B: *This photo shows the remains of Cromwell's head. You were told it was a disgusting tale!*

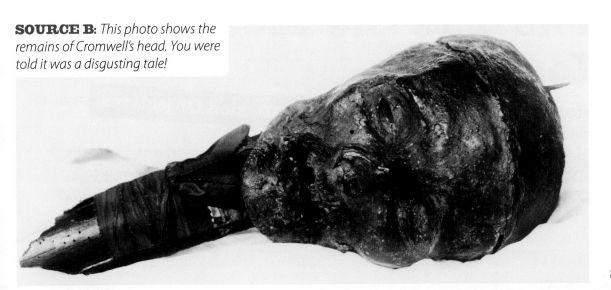

SOURCE C: *This plaque commemorates the burial of Cromwell's head in 1960.*

Near to this place was buried on 25 March 1960 the head of OLIVER CROMWELL Lord Protector of the Commonwealth of England, Scotland & Ireland, Fellow Commoner of this College 1616-7

FACT!

Since Cromwell's death in 1658 there have been 16 British monarchs – four women and twelve men.

What Happened When?

1814

In 1814, when Cromwell's head passed to Josiah Wilkinson, the first plastic surgery was performed in England. Joseph Carpue successfully operated on a British military officer who has lost his nose.

Work

1 a Why was Charles II asked to become king in 1660?
   b What does the word 'regicide' mean?

   c Why do you think Charles II wanted to punish all the men involved in his father's death, including the ones who were already dead?

2 Read the story of Cromwell's head again carefully.
   a Can you suggest reasons why Cromwell's doctors lied about the size of his brain?
   b Why do you think soldier Barnes hid the head?
   c Why do you think Josiah Wilkinson was convinced that he had bought Cromwell's head?
   d What evidence did the doctors have in 1935 that the head was Cromwell's?

   e Why do you think the head was finally buried in secret?

3 Prepare and act out a short role-play called 'The story of Cromwell's head'.
   • Write the script. Remember that you should write the name of the speaker in the margin, and you do not have to use speech marks.
   • Take on some of the roles in the story, such as Wilkinson, Barnes and Russell.
   • Find a suitable 'head' (an old football, perhaps).
   • Act out your role-play in class.

Who was the Merry Monarch?

29 May 1660 was a special day for King Charles II, the son of Charles I. Firstly, it was his 30th birthday. Secondly, it was the day he returned to London after living abroad for almost ten years. Thousands lined the streets of London, Europe's largest city. The country had a king once more.

Mission Objectives

- Explore how, when and why Charles II became king.
- Compare Cromwell's nation with the Merry Monarch's.

SOURCE A: *A painting of the magnificent procession through London to celebrate Charles II's coronation. Can you pick out King Charles II?*

The return of the king

Britain had been without a king since 30 January 1649, the day Charles I was executed. After this, the country was ruled by Parliament for a time and then by Oliver Cromwell, a politician and leader of the army. But Cromwell's strict religious views didn't make him popular. He closed down pubs and theatres and banned most sports. He even banned Christmas and Easter celebrations and replaced them with days of fasting! Before he died in 1658, he picked his son Richard to carry on running the country. But Richard couldn't control the army or Parliament … and didn't really want the job. So, in 1660, Parliament asked Charles I's son to become king – and Britain became a monarchy again.

The Merry Monarch

The new king, Charles II, couldn't have been more different from Cromwell. He brought back all the sports and entertainment that had been banned and soon earned the nickname of 'the Merry Monarch'. Charles himself could often be seen racing down the River Thames in a yacht, gambling on horses at Newmarket, visiting the theatre or playing 'pell mell' (a game combining hockey, golf and croquet) in the streets. Once again, Christmas, May Day and harvest time were celebrated as they were before… and the people loved him for it.

SOURCE B: *King Charles II is offered the first pineapple to have been grown in England, at Dawney Court in Buckinghamshire.*

The serious side

Charles II had a serious side too. He encouraged scientific experiments and loved art, design, mathematics, drama and music. He was also careful to build a good relationship with Parliament because he didn't want there to be another civil war.

Religious freedom?

One of the most positive things about life under Cromwell was that he allowed people to worship in almost any way they wished. King Charles II hoped that there would be some religious freedom too, but Parliament was not so keen. In 1664, they banned any religious services except those of the Church of England, which was now England's official religion.

Carefree... but heir-free!

Charles II was married to a Portuguese princess named Catherine, but had lots of affairs with other women. His mistresses produced 14 (yes, 14!) children between them, but none could be king or queen after Charles' death because he wasn't married to any of their mothers (that was the law). The queen, however, had no children, so when the king died, Charles would be replaced as king by his younger brother, James.

Wise Up Words

monarch   Restoration

SOURCE C: *During Stuart times, the climate was a lot colder than today. As a result, the River Thames often froze solid and frost fairs, like the one shown here, were held on it. Charles II would attend regularly, with his wife and friends. Can you see all the different attractions at this frost fair in 1683?*

Work

1 a Who was the Merry Monarch?
   b Why do you think he was given this nickname?
   c Why would the Merry Monarch always remember 29 May 1660?

2 When Charles II became king in 1660, there were huge parties that went on for many days. List as many reasons as you can why people might have been so happy.

3 Charles II's return as king in 1660 was called the **Restoration**. How do you think it got that name?

4 Explain why Charles II's brother was to become king after Charles's death and not one of the king's children.

5 Look at **Source C**.
   a Make a list of all the different activities you can see. Here are three to start you off:
      • dogs fighting
      • archery
      • a man selling knives and combs.
   b Design an advertising poster for this frost fair. Remember to include:
      • when and where it will take place
      • details of the displays, entertainment and attractions
      • information about who may be attending
      • a picture designed to attract fun-seekers.

A plague is a fast-spreading killer disease. In Tudor and Stuart times, plague struck many times. In 1536, 18,000 people died, 40,000 died in 1603, and 35,000 in 1625. But one of the worst outbreaks during this period happened in 1665. It killed around 70,000 people in London alone and thousands more around the country. It became known as the Great Plague.

Much of what we know about the Great Plague comes from the diary of a man called Samuel Pepys (pronounced 'peeps'). He was a Londoner who wrote in his diary almost every day from 1660 to 1669. His diary (which still survives) tracks the spread of the plague and gives a very personal account of the tragedy. Read some extracts from the diary below.

Mission Objectives

- Explore what people knew about the spread of plague and disease in seventeenth-century London.

SOURCE A: *Samuel Pepys.*

SOURCE B: *Here are some of Pepys' diary entries for the summer of 1665.*

7 June

'The hottest day that I have ever felt in my life. In Drury Lane I saw two or three houses marked with a red cross and the words 'Lord have mercy upon us' written on the door. This worried me so much that I bought a roll of tobacco to smell and chew.'

17 June

'I was riding in a coach through the street when my driver drove slower and slower before stopping. He told me that he felt sick and could hardly see where he was going. I felt very sorry for him – did he have the plague?'

29 June

'I travelled on the river today and saw wagons full of people trying to leave the city. I might move my wife up to Woolwich where there is no plague – but I will remain working in my office. I hear the church bells ring five or six times a day for a funeral.'

20 July

'Walked home past Redriffe, where the sickness is; indeed, it is scattered almost everywhere. 1089 people died of plague this week.'

8 August

'Poor Will, the man who used to sell us ale, his wife and three children died, all of them on the same day. 4000 people died in London this week, 3000 of the plague.'

12 August

'The king and queen are to leave London and go to Salisbury. God preserve us!'

31 August

The mayor said that all fit people should be indoors by 9:00pm, so the sick can exercise and have some fresh air at night.'

3 September

'I bought a new wig but I have been afraid to wear it until now. It might have been made from the hair of a dead plague victim!'

20 September

'What a sad time it is to see no boats on the river; and grass grows all over the roads, and nobody but poor wretches in the streets!'

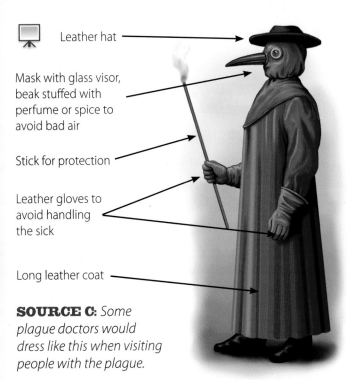

Leather hat

Mask with glass visor, beak stuffed with perfume or spice to avoid bad air

Stick for protection

Leather gloves to avoid handling the sick

Long leather coat

SOURCE C: *Some plague doctors would dress like this when visiting people with the plague.*

FACT!

Samuel Pepys wrote his diary in **shorthand**, a type of coded writing that uses symbols and shortened words that can be written quickly. For years, nobody could work out the codes. Then in 1818, the code was broken by John Smith, who published the Pepys diary in 1825. In 1951, the stories from the diary were made into a muscial called 'And so to bed' – the title came from the way Pepys ended his diary each day.

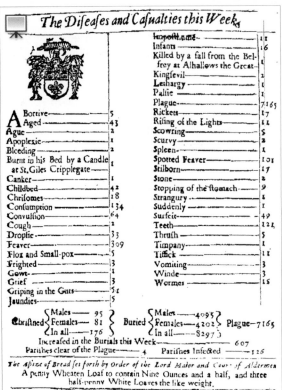

SOURCE D: Searchers *would check each dead body to work out the cause of death. Each week the number of dead and the cause of death were written on a* **Bill of Mortality**. *This one covers 12–19 September 1665.*

People came up with all sorts of suggestions for what caused the plague. Some thought it was caused by the positions of the planets or sent as a punishment from God. Others said it was spread by touching a cat or dog. The most common explanation, though, was that it was caused by bad smells. As a result, it was common for people to smoke a lot, chew tobacco, or carry around bunches of flowers to get rid of the 'bad plague air'! The Mayor of London introduced laws to try and stop the plague – public entertainment was stopped, fires were lit in the streets, dogs and cats were killed and infected houses were sealed up for 40 days …

Work

1 Read the diary again carefully and answer the following questions.
   a What do you think the red crosses and the writing on people's doors meant?
   b Why do you think Samuel Pepys bought a roll of tobacco to smell and chew?
   c How might the plague spread around the country?
   d How did the mayor try to deal with the plague? What do you think his reasons were for doing this?

2 Write a sentence or two to explain each of the following:
   • Bill of Mortality   • searcher

3 Look at **Source C**. Write a sentence or two to explain why the plague doctor is dressed in this way.

4 Look at **Source D** and then answer the following questions.
   a How many people died of the plague?
   b How many people died and were buried 'in all' during this week?
   c Work out what percentage of people were killed by the plague during this week?
   d What do you think is meant by: 'aged', 'grief', 'suddenly', and 'teeth' as causes of death?

Ring a ring o' roses

There are different kinds of plague, each with a different cause. Historians cannot quite agree on the type of plague that hit London in 1665 but most think it was the **bubonic** plague. It gets its name from the 'buboes', or huge round boils which appeared in a victim's armpit or on their groin. There were lots of other nasty **symptoms** too, as you'll find out.

Mission Objectives

- Recall the symptoms of the Great Plague.
- Explore how a nursery rhyme tells us how people tried to avoid catching the plague.

Catching the disease

In 1665, people didn't understand what caused the plague or how to treat it properly. Today, we know most of the answers. We know that the plague was caused by a germ that lived in the guts of fleas. These fleas were carried in the fur of the black rat. A single flea bite caused the plague and usually killed the victim. Historians think that plague-infected rats and fleas brought the disease to England aboard boats bringing goods from the Netherlands. Rats and fleas soon carried the disease all around the filthy streets of London. Towns such as Sunderland, Newcastle and Southampton were also hit by the plague, carried there by people escaping from London and by trading ships.

A nasty nursery rhyme

You will almost certainly have heard or sung the nursery rhyme, 'Ring a ring o' roses'. However, you probably didn't realize how nasty it was when you sang it!

As well as the pus-filled swellings in the victim's armpit and groin, a circular rash of red and black spots appeared all over the body. Some people thought that the rash looked like a red rose. It was common to hear people ask, 'Can you see the mark of a rose on my body yet?' In other words, they wanted to know if they had the rash yet.

A posy is a bunch of flowers. People carried flowers, herbs and spices to make the air around them smell sweeter. Why do you think they wanted to get rid of any bad smells?

Sneezing was one of the first symptoms of the plague. A high temperature, shivering, dizziness, vomiting, and aches and pains would soon follow.

This line speaks for itself. In London alone, it is estimated that over 100,000 people died, but historians can never be sure of the final number. Some deaths were never recorded as caused by the plague because victims' families didn't want their houses sealed up. Thousands were secretly buried in gardens and fields.

Ring a ring o' roses,

A pocket full of posies.

A-tishoo, a-tishoo!

We all fall down.

SOURCE A:
Look carefully at the explanation for each of the lines of the nursery rhyme. They are believed to tell us all sorts of information about the plague.

Month	Number of deaths due to plague – London, 1665
May	43
June	590
July	4117
August	19,046
September	26,219
October	14,373
November	3454
December	590

SOURCE B: *These are* **contemporary** *figures. This means that they are figures from the same period of time. In other words, they were counted up in 1665.*

bubonic   contemporary   symptom

Hungry for More?

There is a second verse to the 'Ring a ring o' roses' rhyme. Find out what it is and try to work out what each line means.

SOURCE C: *Some people spent a fortune on crazy cures for the plague. It's easy to laugh at them now but try to imagine how scared the people must have felt in the summer of 1665. They were obviously willing to try anything!*

Plague Remedies

To avoid the plague:

Place a gold coin in vinegar for one day. Then put the coin in your mouth and keep it there.

If the plague is in your house:

Wrap the victim in woollen blankets, until they are very sweaty. Then cut a live pigeon in half and rub it on the boils. The boils should begin to shrink.

OR

Place a live frog next to a boil. The frog will suck out the poison, swell up and explode.

FACT!

The boys at Eton school in Berkshire were punished if they didn't smoke tobacco. Can you think of any reason why a teacher would want their students to smoke?

Work

1 a What caused the plague?
   b Write down at least five symptoms of the plague.

2 Today, we know how the plague was caused. Look back at Samuel Pepys' diary of 31 August on page 122. Might any of the mayor's actions actually have worked in stopping the spread of disease? Explain your answer carefully.

3 a Using the figures in **Source B**, draw a bar chart to show the number of plague deaths each month in 1665. Remember to give your bar chart a title.
   b According to your graph, how many people died between May and December?
   c If you lived at the time and decided to leave London during the plague, in which month would you have gone and why?

Here comes more trouble!

As you can see from **Source B**, by December 1665, the plague had started to die down. But just as Londoners were beginning to recover from one disaster, another was about to strike … the Great Fire of London!

Who started the Great Fire of London?

In 1666, the London diarist Samuel Pepys was living in Seething Lane, not far from the Tower of London. At three o'clock in the morning on Sunday 2 September, his maid woke him up to tell him about a fire that had started in the city. Pepys got up, looked out of his window and decided that the fire was too far away from him to be worried. So he went back to bed. When Pepys woke later that morning, he took the fire a lot more seriously (see **Source A**).

Mission Objectives

- Describe how the Great Fire devastated London.
- Investigate how and why interpretations the cause of the Great Fire have changed since 1666.
- Evaluate how London was rebuilt after 1666.

▼ **SOURCE A:** *From Samuel Pepys' diary, 1666.*

2 September

'*Walked to the Tower and got up on one of the high places… I did see the houses at the end of the street on fire… The lieutenant of the Tower tells me it began this morning in the king's baker's house in Pudding Lane… we saw the fire grow… in the most horrid, bloody flame, not like the fine flame of an ordinary fire. We stayed till it being darkish, we saw the fire as one entire arch of fire from this to the other side of the bridge, and up the hill for above a mile long. It made me weep to see it. The churches, houses and all on fire, and flaming at once, and a horrid noise the flames made, and the cracking of houses at their ruin. So home with a sad heart.*'

As the day went on, the fire got worse and worse. By midday, 300 houses had been burned down and people were starting to panic. London's buildings were made of wood and the houses were packed close together, so the fire spread quickly – especially as the long, hot summer of 1666 had dried out the timber so that it burned easily.

There was no fire brigade at that time, either. Buckets of water and large metal syringes or 'squirts' were the best the city could offer to fight the fire (see **Source B**).

London's burning

By the evening, the king was so concerned that he ordered houses in the path of the fire to be pulled down. The idea was to create a 'fire break' to stop the fire spreading to more houses. But the man in charge of stopping the fire – the Mayor of London – was struggling with the king's orders. To start with, people didn't want to lose their homes so they only allowed their houses to be pulled down at the last moment. And by then it was too late – the piles of wood and plaster just caught fire too! The mayor himself said, 'I have been pulling down houses, but the fire overtakes us faster than we can do it.'

A city in fear

Strong winds fanned the fire for the next few days – and terrified Londoners fled the city. The streets were full of frightened people, loaded up with all they could carry. Some crafty horse and cart owners charged huge sums of money to desperate homeowners who were trying to empty their houses and take their possessions to safety.

The fire dies down

On Wednesday, the king and his brother brought sailors in to blow up houses with gunpowder. The gaps created by the explosives stopped the fire spreading so quickly and by Thursday the fire was dying down. But the heart of Europe's largest city had been reduced to ashes – 130,000 houses and 88 churches had been destroyed. Around 100,000 people were made homeless. And then the rumours started. Some were saying the fire wasn't an accident at all! So who started the Great Fire of London?

A fire squirt

A leather bucket

A fire hook

SOURCE B: *Firefighting equipment from the 1660s.*

SOURCE C: *This dramatic scene was painted at the time of the fire.*

Work

1 Here is a list of some events during the Great Fire. They're all mixed up. Write down the events in the correct chronological order.
   - Londoners start to leave the city.
   - The fire begins to die down.
   - The king orders houses to be pulled down.
   - Samuel Pepys looks at the fire and goes back to bed.
   - The fire starts.
   - Londoners start to panic.
   - The king and his brother take control and blow up houses.

2 Look at **Source B**.
   a Draw each piece of firefighting equipment.
   b Next to each item, explain why you think it failed to help put out the fire.

3 **a** Why do you think the fire spread so quickly?
   b How was it eventually stopped?

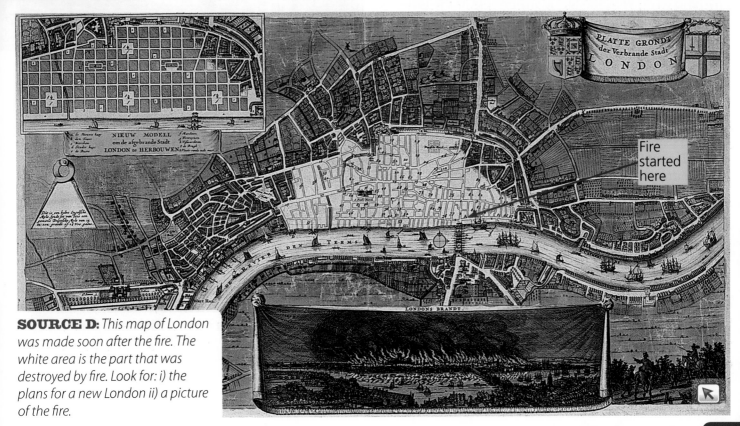

Fire started here

PLATTE GRONDT der Verbrande Stadt LONDON

NIEUW MODELL om de afgebrande Stadt LONDON te HERBOUWEN

LONDONS BRANDT.

SOURCE D: *This map of London was made soon after the fire. The white area is the part that was destroyed by fire. Look for: i) the plans for a new London ii) a picture of the fire.*

So how did the fire start?

The Great Fire of London was a disaster. One person at the time wrote, 'London is no more.' But many people at the time couldn't believe it was an accident. They suspected a plot. Was it the Catholics – perhaps even French Catholics?

In the days immediately after the fire had died down, rumours spread throughout the city and people were attacked at random. A Catholic was nearly beaten to death by a crowd who thought he was carrying fireballs (they were, in fact, tennis balls!). A French visitor was beaten up with an iron bar and another had his furniture smashed up by an angry mob. The mob thought they were both French spies!

Then, a week after the end of the fire, a Frenchman living in London called Robert Hubert was arrested for trying to leave the country – the investigation team suspected he may have been involved in starting the fire. He confessed and then offered to lead the investigation team to where he started the blaze. He was found guilty and hanged on 27 October 1666.

Historians today do not believe that Robert Hubert had anything to do with the fire. Many people at the time thought he did – after all, he was killed for starting it! Clearly, opinions have changed over the past 300 years. So why, and how, are today's views about the start of the fire so different from the views of people in 1666?

SOURCE A: *The monument to the Great Fire. This 61-metre-high column was built in the1670s, near to the site of the baker's shop in Pudding Lane where the fire started. An inscription carved into it at the time (since removed) said that the fire was caused by 'Catholics to introduce the Catholic religion and slavery'. Originally, the monument was to have a statue of King Charles II on top but the king refused. 'After all,' he said, 'I didn't start it.'*

5 November

'Sir Thomas Crew says, from what he has heard at the committee for investigating the burning of the city, that it was certainly done by a plot – it being proved that attempts were made in several places to increase the fire. Both in the city and in the country several Papists [Catholics] boasted that on such a day or in such a time we should find the hottest weather that ever was in England.'

▲ **SOURCE B:** *From Samuel Pepys' diary, 1666.*

'Not many people died as a result of the Great Fire, but one of them was a Frenchman called Robert Hubert. He was found guilty of using gunpowder to start the fire and was hanged in October 1666. Too late, it was discovered that he wasn't even in England when the fire was started.'

▲ **SOURCE C:** *From J. F. Aylett's* In Search of History 1485–1714 *(1984).*

'Robert Hubert, a London watchmaker who was born in France, was tried in October 1666 and executed on the 27th of that month. The only evidence against him was his own confession, which he later denied. It does not appear to be true that he was a Catholic, as was claimed. The fact that he was able to identify the site of the baker's house proved nothing since for a long time it had been on public show. He was in fact mentally disordered and had landed in London from Sweden two days after the fire had started.'

▲ **SOURCE D**: *Robert Latham, a historian, writing in 1974.*

'The summer of 1666 was very hot… at the end of August and the beginning of September a strong easterly wind blew across the city of London drying the old wooden buildings… In the early hours of Sunday, 2 September, a fire broke out in a baker's shop not far from the Tower, and fanned by the strong winds, spread rapidly… Perhaps there was little that anyone could have done: the water pipes were of wood and in any case, the pumping house near London Bridge had been one of the first places to be destroyed… The flames roared along the tunnel-like alleys sweeping up the bone dry houses and exploding when they reached warehouses full of oil, tar, spirits and other inflammable materials. Near blazing churches, molten lead ran like water down the gutters.'

▲ **SOURCE E**: *From Peter Moss' History Alive Book 1 (1980).*

'The fire started in the king's bakery run by Thomas Farynor in Pudding Lane. Farynor denied this at the time and a deluded French watchmaker called Robert Hubert claimed he did it. Although it was evident to judge and jury that he couldn't have done it, they hanged him anyway. His corpse was torn apart by an angry mob, suspecting a Popish [Catholic] plot. Justice wasn't done until 1986, when the Worshipful Company of Bakers [a kind of Baker's society] claimed official responsibility and apologised for the fire.'

▲ **SOURCE F**: *From* The Book of General Ignorance *by John Lloyd and John Mitchinson (2006).*

FACT!

With the fire fast approaching, Samuel Pepys rushed to save some of his precious belongings from the inferno by burying them in his garden – including a big piece of cheese.

Work

 The Big Write!

 Use all the evidence to help you to work out who started the Great Fire of London. Was it a Catholic or French plot, or simply an unfortunate accident?

1 Find evidence of a plot.

Look at **Sources A** to **F** and make notes on which sources support the theory that it was a plot to burn down London. Who could have done this? Which sources support the idea of a plot?

2 Find sources to suggest the fire was an accident.

Perhaps the fire was an accident? Make notes on the sources that support this idea. Where could the fire have started? Why did it spread so quickly? Write down your findings.

3 Think – which sources can you trust?

Can you rely on some sources more than others? Which sources might it be wrong to trust? Why do so many of the modern sources disagree with sources from the time of the fire? Why do you think Catholics were blamed by some people? Write down your opinions.

4 It's time to reveal your findings.

Write a paragraph to explain how you think the Great Fire of London started. Remember to back up your theories with the evidence provided!

What was so special about the Great Fire?

The Great Fire is important for a number of reasons. To start with, the fact that a French Catholic was hanged for starting the fire – and he wasn't even in the country when it began – shows just how much many ordinary people didn't like the French or Catholics at this time! Catholics all over London were beaten up by angry mobs, indicating just how paranoid Londoners were about a 'Catholic plot'.

But the Great Fire is hugely significant for another reason too. To put it simply, the fire is important because it destroyed London! Before the Great Fire, most of London was a filthy, stinking maze of streets and alleys full of dirt and disease. Fire destroyed five-sixths of the buildings within the city walls and planning for the rebuilding of the city began soon after the fire was finally out.

New plans

The king asked for plans for a new city and within two weeks an **architect** called Christopher Wren had written up his ideas. He planned a city with broad, straight streets, wide-open spaces and magnificent new brick or stone churches and homes.

Despite Wren's ideas for a magnificent new city, most of them were ignored. The people whose homes had been destroyed wanted them built quickly and in exactly the same places as their old ones. Few people wanted to – or could afford to – give up their land to make London a nicer place to live. However, the king insisted on some changes (See **Source B**).

> ### FACT!
> Insurance companies started up as a result of the Great Fire. Before the fire, if your house burned down, you paid for it to be rebuilt. From 1666 onwards, a house owner could pay small sums of money to insure their property. If a fire started, the employees of the insurance company would put out the fire using their own fire engine.

SOURCE A: *The architect, Sir Christopher Wren (1632–1723), had grand plans for rebuilding London after the Great Fire.*

New ideas

New regulations for New London

- Building new homes out of wood is BANNED.
- All new houses should be built of BRICK or STONE.
- All new streets must be WIDE.
- Houses over 9m wide are only allowed on main streets.
- 100 existing streets must be WIDENED.
- The filthy Fleet River will be covered over and some new common sewers will be built.

▲ **SOURCE B:** *New rules for a new city.*

SOURCE C: *People would display a **fire mark** on the outside of their house to prove their insurance fees had been paid.*

SOURCE D: *St Paul's Cathedral is still a dominant part of the landscape in modern London.*

SOURCE E: *St Paul's Cathedral is shown here in 1747.*

A new city

By 1676, a new city had risen from the ashes. London looked like it had been planned properly – rows of houses, all the same height, made from the same building materials. Cleaner streets meant fewer rats and fleas. Stone buildings meant less chance of fire. Never again was there a plague or fire on the same scale as the ones of 1665 and 1666.

One of Wren's ideas that everyone loved was his plan for more than 50 new churches. The most famous, St Paul's Cathedral, took 35 years to build (See **Sources D** and **E**). By the time he died in 1723, Wren had been asked to build other magnificent buildings, including colleges and hospitals.

> ### FACT!
>
> Wren is buried in St Paul's. If you visit his grave, you will find the words 'Si monumentum requiris, circumspice' – they mean, 'If you seek his monument, look around you.'

Work

1 a How much of London was destroyed by the Great Fire?

 b What sort of new city did Christopher Wren plan? Give reasons for his ideas.

 c Why were some of his plans not used?

 d Do you think the inscription on Wren's grave is an appropriate one?

2 a Explain the phrase 'blessing in disguise'. You might like to discuss this with a classmate.

 b How might the Great Fire of London be seen as a blessing in disguise?

3 Look at **Source C**.

 a What is insurance?

 b Explain why insurance companies introduced fire marks.

What about the women?

Some of the most famous people in Tudor and Stuart history were women: Elizabeth I and Mary Queen of Scots, for example. But what about other women? How were they treated? What was everyday life like for them? Let's look for some answers.

Mission Objectives

- Compare the lives of rich and poor women in Tudor and Stuart times.
- Explore how some men treated their wives.

A hard life

Like poor men, poor women faced tough lives. In fact, their lives remained much the same as they had been for women in the Middle Ages. Almost 95 per cent of the population still lived in the countryside and the women worked just as hard as the men (see **Source A**).

The dangers of childbirth

Regardless of whether you were rich or poor at this time, having children was particularly dangerous. People didn't know that germs caused illness, and women often gave birth in filthy conditions – dirty water, filthy rags, no disinfectant, and no antibiotics. Babies often died soon after they were born and one in every five births ended with the death of the mother.

Historians can find out a lot more about richer women, but being wealthy didn't always mean that their lives were a lot better than poorer women's. Read the extracts in **Source C**, which were written by Samuel Pepys, a London gentleman who famously kept a diary during Stuart times. His wife was called Elizabeth.

'… get up, clean the clothes, milk the cows, collect eggs, feed the pigs, dress the children, prepare food, bake bread, brew ale, make butter and cheese, mend clothes, go to market, sell butter, cheese and eggs…'

▲ **SOURCE A:** *A farmer describes his wife's day in 1562.*

SOURCE B: *This picture shows the inside of a country cottage.*

Be a Top Historian

Historians know less about poorer women than they do about the richer women. Most of the poor couldn't read or write letters or keep diaries for us to study years later. Richer women are easier to find out about. They wrote to friends, kept diaries, allowed themselves to be painted and sometimes earned so much money that they had to pay taxes, which were recorded.

2 May 1663

'Slept until 7 o'clock, then up to my office. Argued with my wife about her not keeping the house clean. I called her a "beggar" and she called me a "prick louse".'

19 December 1664

'I was angry with my wife for not telling the servants what to do properly. She gave me an angry answer so I hit her over the left eye, such a blow as the poor wretch did cry out. She then scratched and bit me.'

▲ **SOURCE C:** *Extracts from Samuel Pepys' diary.*

A woman's life

Many women, especially those from wealthier families, had their husbands chosen for them by their parents. And husbands had a lot of power over their wives. For instance, a 'nagging' wife could find herself on the **ducking stool**. She would be tied to a stool and lowered into the local pond as punishment. If that didn't work, she may even be forced to wear a **scold's bridle** for a day or so – an iron mask was put over the woman's head, with a piece of metal that went into her mouth to hold her tongue down and stop her talking. The husband would then lead her around on a leash to show other men that he had her under control.

Women were not allowed to divorce their husbands but even if they could have done so, they wouldn't have been able to take any of their property with them. The law stated that once a woman was married, everything she owned became her husband's. Men, however, were allowed to divorce their wives. One kind of divorce was a **wife sale** in which men were allowed to sell off their wives.

As you can see, many women lived tough lives but some visitors to this country thought differently. The writer of **Source F** thought that wealthy women were still better off than women from other countries.

> '*Wives in England are in the power of their husbands, but they are not kept as strictly as in Spain. Nor are they shut up… They go to market, are well dressed. Some take it easy and leave the care of the household to their servants… They spend time walking and riding, playing cards and visiting friends, talking to neighbours and making merry with them at childbirths and christenings. All this with the permission of their husbands… This is why England is called the paradise of married women.*'

▲ **SOURCE F:** Written by a male visitor from the Netherlands in 1575.

Read **Source C** again. It is from the diary of Samuel Pepys. Imagine that Elizabeth Pepys kept a diary too. Write her diary entries for 2 May and 19 December. She would probably have had a different view of the incidents!

Hungry for More?

Wise Up Words

ducking stool   scold's bridle   wife sale

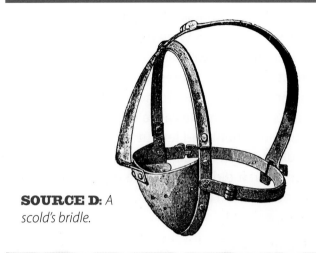

SOURCE D: *A scold's bridle.*

> '*He put a rope around her neck and led her to the market place. He put her up to be sold to the highest bidder, as if she were a horse. A buyer is usually arranged beforehand.*'

▲ **SOURCE E:** *This description of a 'wife sale' was written in 1700.*

Work

1. ✏ Write a sentence or two to explain the following:
   - ducking stool · scold's bridle · wife sale

2. Look at **Source B**.
   a. There are three people in the picture. What are they doing?
   b. Look at the woman cleaning clothes on the table. Describe the sort of day you think she was having. Use **Source A** to help you.
   c. How has cooking and washing changed since then?

3. a. Why do you think one in five births ended with the death of the mother?
   b. How are conditions different today?

4. Read **Source F**.
   a. Do you think the visitor was describing the lives of rich or poor English women? Give reasons for your answer.
   b. He describes England at this time as 'the paradise of married women'. Do you agree? Give reasons for your answer, using evidence from these pages.

Can you cure King Charles II?

In Stuart times, approaches to medicine were a combination of different ideas. Some were very clever… but others were just crazy! Some doctors were beginning to work out exactly how the human body worked. Others hadn't got a clue! One of the most widely used cures was 'bloodletting'. This was based on an old Greek and Roman idea that too much blood in a person's body was the cause of their illness. The answer was to cut the patient and let out the 'bad blood'. Soon their body would be back 'in balance' again. Needless to say, it didn't work, but it didn't stop some of the country's most famous doctors from trying it.

Mission Objectives

- Evaluate the various treatments on offer to King Charles II and make decisions about what to do.

The king is ill

At 8:00am on 2 February 1685, Charles II fainted. It was soon clear that he was very ill. A dozen doctors gathered around his body. This was their chance to prove themselves as great doctors. If they could save him they would be richly rewarded. Fail, and the king might die – and nobody wanted the blame for that!

Like all doctors, they had a choice of treatments. Imagine that you are one of the king's doctors. You will be given a series of choices to make, based on real treatments available at the time.

Can you cure King Charles II?

What to do:

1 Read each of the '**How's he feeling?**' boxes carefully. They will give you some idea of the king's condition.

2 Choose a treatment from the list. You must have a good reason for your choice.

3 Record your choices and make a note of the reason.

4 Now work out your score. Get your list of decisions and go through the score card. Would you have made a successful doctor in Stuart England?

Day 1: 2 February 1685
How's he feeling? After collapsing, the king has been unconscious for two hours. As the doctors arrive, he begins to wake up. He is in pain.

Treatment 1: What do you do?
Do you:
a open up a vein in his arm and drain some blood, then make him vomit?
b do nothing and wait to see if he gets any better?
c wash his hair in urine?

> He's just as bad. You must keep trying.

Treatment 2: What will you do next?
Do you:
a bleed him again, perhaps a little blood from his shoulder this time?
b shave his head and burn his scalp to make it blister?
c pray?

Day 2: 3 February 1685
How's he feeling? The king is speaking again but still feels poorly. He still faints occasionally but recovers sooner than the day before.

Treatment 3: What do you do?
Do you:
a suggest injecting him with **antibiotics**?
b drain more blood and then pump a liquid up his bottom to make him empty his bowels?
c leave him alone, he seems better today – perhaps he is recovering?

Day 3: 4 February 1685
How's he feeling? He wakes up bright and early but collapses again at dinnertime. He seems to be getting worse.

Treatment 4: What do you do?
Do you:
a bleed him again – more than you have already?
b give him powdered human skull in a sweet drink? This is viewed by many as a super cure for any illness.
c call another doctor. Perhaps he can help more than you? Some people are saying that herbal remedies can work really well.

Day 4: 5 February 1685
How's he feeling? The king is getting worse. He collapses again. He sometimes cries out in pain. The doctors are very frustrated.

Treatment 5: What do you do?
Do you:
a mash up the brain of a young man who has died violently, add some wine and horse dung, and pour this over the king's body?
b carry out more bleeding and perhaps give him a **laxative** to empty his bowels?
c force him to eat Peruvian tree bark, a medicine used for fevers?

Score card

Use this score card to work out your points for the doctor task. When you have your final score, look at the 'How did you get on?' box and see if you would make a good Stuart doctor.

Treatment 1

a Yes, this is what the doctors did: 5 points.

b You must do something – you are one of the king's doctors – you can't just sit there: 0 points.

c Don't be silly, this is a Stuart cure for ringworm. It might be worth a try though: 3 points.

Treatment 2

a This is what the doctors did. Bloodletting was the key to success… or so they thought: 5 points.

b The doctors did this too. Good thinking: 5 points.

c Not a bad idea, perhaps God would help him: 2 points.

Treatment 3

a Antibiotics? They've not been invented yet. Nobody knows what you are talking about. Be careful, some people might think you are a witch: 0 points.

b Good idea. This is what the king's doctors did: 5 points.

c Sounds sensible doesn't it? But you are missing a day's bleeding: 0 points.

Treatment 4

a Not a bad idea, but if you bleed too much you might put him 'out of balance' again: 3 points.

b This is what the doctors did: 5 points.

c Get another doctor! Don't be ridiculous. The king's doctors know what they are doing (even if he's not getting better!): 0 points.

Treatment 5

a A good treatment, but one for the plague. Perhaps worth a try, though: 3 points.

b Another good treatment, perhaps tomorrow?: 2 points.

c This is what the doctors did: 5 points.

Treatment 6

a A common treatment for toothache. The king doesn't seem to have toothache, but you never know: 2 points.

b This is what the doctors did: 5 points.

c You can't stop treating him, he's the king! 0 points.

Day 5: 6 February 1685

How's he feeling? The king is still getting worse. The doctors think there is great danger that he may die. Perhaps there is one last chance?

Treatment 6: What do you do?

Do you:

a cut his gums open with a new nail and then hammer the nail into an old oak tree?

b give him some oriental bezoar stone, a substance found in the stomachs of Persian goats? Added to wine, it should stop all poisons.

c stop treating him; nothing you do seems to have any effect?

STOP PRESS … STOP PRESS … STOP PRESS … STOP PRESS …

The king is dead. Shortly after noon he collapsed for the last time. The doctors failed to keep him alive.

How did you get on?

If you scored 20 or more:

You would have made a very successful doctor in Stuart England. However, you may have killed a lot of patients!

11–19:

You would have made a good Stuart doctor. However, you've still got a lot to learn. Some of your treatments were clever, others were just crazy!

10 or below:

You would have failed as a Stuart doctor. You seem to know nothing about treating people. However, if the real doctors hadn't taken so much blood, the king might have lived longer…

Wise Up Words

antibiotic   bloodletting   laxative

FACT!

Years later, it was discovered that the king had a kidney disease. The last thing that Charles needed was the bloodletting treatment. In fact, losing blood is the worst treatment a kidney patient can receive. His doctors actually shortened his life.

Work

1 What is bloodletting? Why did doctors use this treatment?

2 Think carefully. Why do you think some of the treatments used by the king's doctors were so bizarre?

3 One of the king's doctors was Sir Charles Scarburgh. Write a letter to a friend, imagining you are Sir Charles, explaining how you treated the king and why… and what happened to him. Remember to follow the conventions of a letter, such as including your address, your friend's address, and the date.

The Glorious Revolution

When Charles II died in 1685, he left 14 children behind. So, surely one of them would become king or queen after his death, right? Wrong! Despite having lots of children, none of them were with his wife, the queen. So they weren't allowed, by law, to inherit the throne. So who became monarch after Charles II's death? What happened as a result? And how did it all lead to a revolution?

Mission Objectives

- Recall the main events that led to the return of a Protestant monarchy.
- Examine the reasons why the monarchy changed from Catholic to Protestant.
- Evaluate the changes that William and Mary agreed to.

A new king

After the death of Charles II, his younger brother James became King James II. He was a Catholic… but most people in Britain weren't. In fact, there hadn't been a Catholic monarch since the time of 'Bloody Mary' over 100 years before. Some people worried that James might try to make everyone in the country Catholic and that this might lead to some sort of religious war. Other people weren't worried at all about the Catholic king. James was quite old and his only children, Mary and Anne, were Protestants. It was thought that King James might die soon and then his eldest daughter, Mary, would take over and everything would carry on as before. But things didn't go to plan…

James makes waves

Soon after James became king he started to change things – lots of things! This really worried some of the leading politicians in Parliament. Look at the cartoons and see if you can work out why.

James used his power to give lots of the top jobs in the army and in government to Catholics.

James built up a large army, even though there wasn't a war on. Could he be planning to use it against Parliament, just like his father Charles I had done in the Civil War?

James said in a speech made in 1687 that he wished all his subjects were Catholics. Many people felt threatened by this – was he planning to turn the country Catholic again?

In 1687, James lost patience with Parliament and closed it down. He was behaving exactly like his father Charles I – and we all know how that ended!

In 1688, the unthinkable happened! James' new Catholic wife gave birth to a baby boy. As he was male, he pushed past James' daughters to be next in line to the throne. It looked like the country would continue to have a Catholic king after James' death.

A step too far?

The birth of King James' baby boy was too much for Parliament. The new prince would be brought up as a Catholic… and so would his sons, and so on. Parliament feared that the country would have a Catholic king for ever more. And Parliament, made up mostly of Protestants, didn't want this – so they decided to do something about it!

What Happened When? 1687

In 1687, the same year that James II closed down Parliament, scientist Isaac Newton published his important and influential books commonly known as *Principia*. These texts helped give many scientists a much better understanding of physics and the nature of the universe.

Be a Top Historian

Top historians know that most events have a number of **causes**. Howvver, there's usually one that finally triggers an event. Try to decide which you think was the most important cause of the Glorious Revolution

Wise Up Words

Bill of Rights

SOURCE A: *King James II was the first Catholic monarch in over 100 years.*

James' new son is often called 'the warming-pan baby'. Find out why… it's a fascinating story!

Hungry for More?

Work

1 Why did none of Charles II's children become king or queen after his death?

2 When James became king, why were some people:
   a worried about this?
   b not worried about this?

3 Which of James' actions upset Parliament the most? Copy the following sentences, placing them in the order you think would have caused most alarm. Write a conclusion explaining why you have chosen the order you have.
   - He dissolved Parliament.
   - He gave all the top jobs to Catholics.
   - He created his own army.
   - His wife gave birth to a son.
   - He wished that all the people in England were Catholic.

The Glorious Revolution

Dastardly daughter?

In the summer of 1688, a plot was hatched by some leading Protestants to get rid of Catholic King James. The plan was for Mary, the king's eldest daughter, and her Protestant husband, William of Orange, to gather an army and fight James. They would then become joint king and queen. That's right – the plan was for Mary to fight her dad. She agreed, with the full support of her husband, who was a member of the ruling family of the Netherlands.

The future's orange!

Mary and William's army landed in Devon on 5 November 1688, having crossed the sea from the Netherlands. King James got an army ready to fight, but John Churchill, one of his key generals, swapped sides and joined Mary and William. James realized that he couldn't beat his daughter's army and fled to France. In fact, there wasn't any fighting at all, but a revolution had taken place. One ruler had been replaced by another! Protestants called this the Glorious Revolution.

Rules for William and Mary

Parliament then invited William and Mary to become king and queen, ruling together. They accepted the offer, but had to agree to some conditions (see **Source B**). In the past, some kings had been able to rule without consulting Parliament at all. As a result, Parliament was especially keen that this didn't happen again. So William and Mary also had to agree to involve Parliament in the running of the country and to consult them at least every three years.

FACT!

To reward John Churchill for changing sides, William made him Earl of Marlborough. John Churchill was the great, great, great, great, great, great grandfather of Sir Winston Churchill, Britain's prime minister during the Second World War.

FACT!

Mary refused to be queen unless her husband was made king… and William refused to accept any sort of position where his wife was in a higher position – so they really were joint rulers!

SOURCE A: *William of Orange lands at Torbay, Devon in 1688.*

The Bill of Rights

We promise to allow:

1 *Parliament to make all the laws*

2 *Parliament to decide on taxes*

3 *Parliament to share control of the army*

4 *Members of Parliament to say what they want*

5 *all trials to go ahead without any interference from the king or queen*

6 *no Catholic kings or queens ever again.*

Signed William & Mary

SOURCE B: *This agreement, which William and Mary had to sign, was known as the **Bill of Rights**.*

SOURCE D: *A silver medal from the time when William and Mary ruled together.*

A turning point

These agreements were a turning point in British history. The struggle between Parliament and the monarchy was finally over. Parliament had won! It had real power and was now more powerful than any king or queen. Monarchs could now be appointed by Parliament and had to stick to the rules that Parliament created.

Work

1 Put the following events in the correct chronological order. You might want to draw a storyboard to illustrate them.
   - William lands in Devon with 12,000 soldiers.
   - James flees to France.
   - James' wife has a son.
   - Important Protestants invite William to invade.
   - The leader of James' army joins William and Mary.

2 a Why do you think Mary agreed to help overthrow her father?
   b Why do you think William and Mary chose 5 November as the date to land in England to remove the Catholic king?

3 Imagine you are a Protestant plotter. Write a letter to William and Mary detailing your plan and asking them for their help. Give reasons for your actions and why you think your idea is a good one. Remember to follow the conventions of a letter, such as including your address, the recipient's address, and the date.

4 The Glorious Revolution is sometimes called the Bloodless Revolution. Why do you think it was given this other name?

5 a Why do you think Parliament made William and Mary agree to the changes they did? Copy out the list of promises and alongside each one, say why you think Parliament wanted William and Mary to agree to it.
   b Do you think these changes were for the better? Give reasons for your answer.

Exit the Stuarts... enter the Georgians

William and Mary became joint king and queen in 1689. But they didn't enjoy an easy reign. There were rebellions in both Ireland and Scotland, which were eventually stopped with great force by William's army. So what exactly happened in Ireland and Scotland? What became of William and Mary? And who ruled after their deaths?

Mission Objectives

- Investigate the consequences of the Glorious Revolution.
- Explain the official establishment of the United Kingdom.

Irish issues

English kings and queens had always tried to control Ireland. Brutal English armies had invaded many times, but the Irish remained determined to keep the English out. They failed. When old King James II, who had fled to France in 1688, landed in Ireland in 1689 and gathered a Catholic army, William sent in the troops. At the Battle of the Boyne in 1690, James' forces were crushed. William took away lots of land from Irish Catholics and gave it to English Protestants. Strict laws were introduced too, banning Irish Catholics from teaching, voting or carrying a sword. The deep divisions in Ireland between Catholics and Protestants created at this time still live on today.

Scottish scrapping

There was rebellion in Scotland too. Many Scots supported old King James II, especially in the mountainous areas called the Highlands. In an attempt to settle things, William asked all the important Scottish families (known as clans) to swear an oath of loyalty to him. But one clan – the MacDonalds of Glencoe – missed the deadline for the oath. So William ordered that they all be killed. In total, 38 members of the MacDonald clan were massacred in 1692 – an act of violence that is still remembered in Scotland today.

William all alone

In 1694, Mary died of smallpox, leaving William to rule alone. As they had no children, Parliament passed a law which named Mary's sister, Anne, as the next ruler. William died in 1702… and Anne became queen.

SOURCE A: *This memorial is situated on the site of the 1692 Massacre of Glencoe in the Highlands of West Scotland.*

FACT!

William was devastated by Mary's death. When he died, he was wearing her wedding ring and a locket containing some of her hair.

Queen Anne

Anne was the sister of Queen Mary (William's wife), the daughter of James II, niece of Charles II and granddaughter of Charles I. She gave birth to 17 children. Tragically, all of them died before she became queen. Parliament was worried that if she died without an heir, the throne might pass to her younger brother, who was a Catholic. So they passed a law called the **Act of Settlement**, which stated that after Anne's death the throne would pass to the nearest Protestant heir.

United Kingdom

In order to make the country even more secure, Parliament passed the **Act of Union** in 1707. This meant that England, Wales, and now Scotland, were united, with one Parliament based in London. Ireland was also largely under English control by then. So Queen Anne was the first monarch to officially call herself Queen of Great Britain and Ireland.

German George

Queen Anne died in 1714. Her closest Protestant relation was a man called George from Hanover, which is now an area of Germany. As a result of spending all his life abroad, he couldn't speak English! He became Britain's king on 1 August 1714. So Anne was the last ruler from the Stuart family… and German George had now taken over!

SOURCE C:

King George I never learned to speak English and spent lots of his time in Hanover. He mainly left Parliament alone to run the country… which they liked, of course!

Wise Up Words

Act of Settlement   Act of Union

SOURCE B: *A portrait of Queen Anne, the last Stuart monarch. She was a rather large lady – in fact, when she died people said that her coffin was nearly square.*

Work

1. Construct a timeline with the title 'Uniting the United Kingdom'. Mark the following dates on your timeline. Then add a few sentences to explain the importance of each date.
   - 1689
   - 1690
   - 1692
   - 1694
   - 1702
   - 1707
   - 1714

2. Complete the following sentences.
   a. Charles II was James II's (uncle/father/brother).
   b. James II was Queen Mary's (uncle/father/brother).
   c. James II was Queen Anne's (uncle/father/brother).
   d. Queen Anne was Queen Mary's (sister/mother/niece).

3. What methods were used to make sure Ireland and Scotland came under English control?

4. In your own words, explain why a German man became King of Great Britain.

The Battle of Culloden

What do you think of when you hear the word 'Jacobite'? Is it a strange alien invader in an episode of *Doctor Who* or a unit of computer memory, like a megabyte or a gigabyte? In fact, Jacobite is the name given to a group of people who rebelled against the new monarch, King George I. So what were they so upset about? How much of a threat were they? And where did the name 'Jacobite' come from?

Mission Objectives

- Define the word 'Jacobite'.
- Examine the Jacobite Rebellions of 1715 and 1745.
- Explain why Bonnie Prince Charlie was a threat to the Georgians.

In 1714, Queen Anne died. She was replaced as monarch by her closest *Protestant* relation. He was a German named George, who became King George I. But many people weren't happy with this. They wanted Anne's half-brother James to be king instead. The people who supported James (who was living in France) were called Jacobites because the Latin for James is *Jacobus*.

The first Jacobite Rebellion

The reason why James wasn't king in the first place was because he was a Catholic… and Catholics were banned from being King or Queen of Great Britain (they still are!). This was why James' father, King James II, was removed from the throne in 1688 and replaced by Protestant rulers, William and Mary. And Queen Anne (who followed William and Mary) had been a Protestant too… and so was King George I.

But James had strong support, particularly in Scotland, and decided to rebel against King George. In 1715, James landed in Peterhead, Scotland and gathered an army. But his army was soon defeated and James ran off to Rome. He never returned to Britain.

The second Jacobite Rebellion

Thirty years later, James' son Charles tried to take the British throne. Charles, known as Bonnie Prince Charlie, had been brought up in Rome and had never been to Britain. But when he landed in Scotland in July 1745, he claimed 'I am home'!

Bonnie Prince Charlie soon won control of Scotland and headed into England. He got as far as Derby, 130 miles from London, but failed to get the support that he'd hoped for. As a result, he and his men were forced to march back to Scotland… with King George's soldiers chasing them.

SOURCE A: *The Jacobites got as far south as Derby but then had to retreat and fought their last battle against the king's army at Culloden.*

The Battle of Culloden

Eventually, in April 1746, the king's army caught up with Charlie and the Jacobites at Culloden. The Jacobites were outnumbered two to one, poorly armed and half-starving… and were beaten by the king's forces. Charlie escaped from the battlefield – just – but was hunted all over Scotland (see **Source C**). Eventually, he escaped to France, dressed as a woman… and never again returned to Britain. He spent another 42 years living unhappily abroad and once said, 'I should have died with my men at Culloden.'

SOURCE D: *Charlie was hunted around Scotland for five months. He was eventually rowed in a small boat to the Isle of Skye by a woman called Flora MacDonald. Then he was taken to France. This traditional ballad commemorates these events.*

Chorus:
Speed, bonnie boat, like a bird on the wing,
Onward! the sailors cry;
Carry the lad that's born to be king
Over the sea to Skye.
Loud the winds howl, loud the waves roar,
Thunderclouds rend the air;
Baffled, our foes stand by the shore,
Follow they will not dare.

[Chorus]
Though the waves leap, so soft shall ye sleep,
Ocean's a royal bed.
Rocked in the deep, Flora will keep
Watch by your weary head.

[Chorus]
Many's the lad fought on that day,
Well the Claymore could wield,
When the night came, silently lay
Dead in Culloden's field.

[Chorus]
Burned are their homes, exile and death
Scatter the loyal men;
Yet ere the sword cool in the sheath
Charlie will come again.

PRINCE CHARLES EDWARD
After Richard Cooper, Edinburgh, 1745
From a coloured Engraving in the collection of W. B. Blaikie

▲ **SOURCE B:** *The Battle of Culloden was the last battle fought on British soil. Interestingly, people think of Culloden as a battle between Scotland and England. But more Scots fought on the king's side than on Bonnie Prince Charlie's. Charlie was helped by Catholic French soldiers sent by his ally, the King of France.*

◀ **SOURCE C:** *This 'wanted' poster for Charlie was published when he was on the run in 1746. The reward for catching him was £30,000 (almost £4 million today).*

Work

1 What was a Jacobite?

2 What were the similarities and differences between the first and second Jacobite Rebellions?

3 Name one thing that makes the Battle of Culloden significant.

4 Look at **Source D**.
   a What does the song commemorate?
   b Do you think it was written by a supporter of Bonnie Prince Charlie, or not? Explain your answer.

5 Look at **Source C**. Create your own wanted poster for Bonnie Prince Charlie. Before you start, think about all the things that should be included. You might want to brainstorm this as a class… or carry out some extra research on him.

What does Robert know that John didn't?

The 1600s and 1700s was a great age of exploration and discovery. Scientists and doctors, for example, no longer accepted some of the old beliefs and tried out new theories and methods that they hoped would shed new light on some of the mysteries of the world (and the universe!). Lots and lots of new ideas about health, mathematics, politics, science and astronomy were discussed at this time – and many exciting new experiments and discoveries took place. But what impact would all this have on two ordinary gentlemen like John and Robert?

Mission Objectives

- Examine the difference between the Age of Faith and the Age of Reason.
- Explore some of the key discoveries, theories and inventions of the sixteenth, seventeenth and early eighteenth centuries.

Step 1

Meet John, a well-educated Tudor gentleman who lived around the time that Henry VIII became king in 1509. Have a look at his views, ideas and beliefs about the world… and universe!

The Earth (which I know is round!) is at the centre of the universe. The Sun, other planets and stars move around the Earth in perfect circles.

The study of the stars and planets is very important. Astrology even helps doctors know when to treat you because different groups of stars rule different parts of your body!

Books are becoming more and more popular, mainly because they are cheaper and cover all sorts of wonderful topics. The invention of the printing press in 1450 has changed everything. Now ideas and information can spread quickly.

All living things are made up of a mixture of the four elements — earth, air, fire and water. The Ancient Greeks believed this… and so do we!

Today's doctors rely on ancient books written by Greek and Roman writers. They explain how the body works. For example, I know that the body burns up blood like fuel and new blood is made in the liver.

I also know that the human body is made up of four substances — blood, phlegm, yellow bile and black bile. These are sometimes called the four humours. And if a person is ill, it's because their humours are out of balance. So, if you've got a fever and you're hot and sweaty, it means you've got too much blood in your body… so your doctor will bleed you. Then you'll be back in balance again!

The king is the ruler of this country. He makes all the big decisions and no one messes with him. Advisors help him and he has to consult Parliament from time to time… but us ordinary folk know our place!

God controls everything — bad harvests, plagues, good harvests, births, deaths… it's all God's work (or the Devil's!). And the best way to find out about the world is to study the Bible and attend church.

Step 2

Now you've met John and got to know him a little, take a journey through some of the great advances, new ideas and major discoveries of the next 250 years.

SOURCE A: *The universe according to Copernicus. Note: i) the Sun at the centre; ii) the planets (including Earth) circling the Sun; iii) the moon circling Earth; iv) the signs of the zodiac around the edge of the map – many believed that the signs of the zodiac affected life on Earth in some way.*

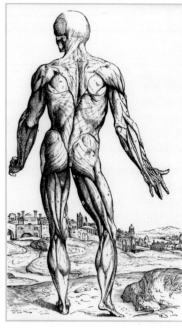

SOURCE B: *An illustration from Vesalius' book.*

1543

The ideas of Polish **astronomer**, Nicolaus Copernicus, are published. He used mathematics to work out that the Sun – and not the Earth – was the centre of the universe. He proposed that the Earth and all the other planets move around the Sun… and that the moon moves around the Earth.

1543

In Italy, a doctor called Andreas Vesalius published some of the first accurate drawings of the human body (see **Source B**). He robbed cemeteries to get the bodies of executed criminals so he could study them, and conducted experiments which proved some of the ancient medieval theories were wrong.

1575

A French army surgeon, Ambroise Paré, used bandages and soothing ointments (rather than boiling oil) to treat wounds and prevent infection.

1609

An Italian, Galileo Galilei, made the first practical telescope and saw planets such as Mars and Venus for the first time. However, when he said he could prove that the Earth moved around the Sun, the Church rejected this idea… and made him deny his theory in public!

'The moon isn't smooth; it's rough, full of cavities [holes], like the face of the Earth.'

SOURCE C: *Galileo, 1610.*

1620

The British politician and scientist, Francis Bacon, came up with a new way of carrying out scientific experiments. One of the main methods of solving a scientific problem (since ancient times) had been for clever men to discuss it until they all agreed. Bacon said this was *not* the way to do science. He said that if a person wanted to know about the world, they had to study it and experiment – a lot. Bacon's ideas inspired many, many scientists, including Isaac Newton and Robert Boyle.

SOURCE D: *Francis Bacon made a lasting impact on science.*

1628

English doctor, William Harvey, proved that the heart is a pump and circulates blood around the body (see **Source A**). Soon after, doctors began to experiment with blood transfusions.

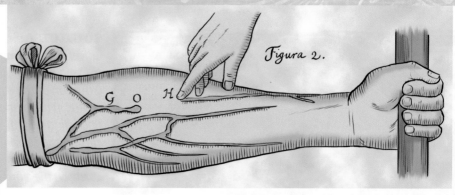

Figura 2.

1655

Dutchman Christiaan Huygens made big improvements to telescopes and was able to see planets more clearly than ever before.

SOURCE A: *A blood flow diagram from a book Harvey wrote. By cleverly experimenting on the veins in people's arms, Harvey proved that the heart pumps blood around the body.*

SOURCE B: *Newton's picture used to appear on £1 notes. These were replaced by £1 coins in 1988.*

1657

Christopher Wren (best known for designing St Paul's Cathedral, London) was appointed Professor of Astronomy at Gresham College, London. Wren's first love was science and maths, and he had already invented an instrument that wrote in the dark, a weather clock and a new language for the deaf. He met regularly with other scientists and mathematicians. This group would eventually become the Royal Society (see **1662**).

1661

In London, Robert Boyle proves that air is essential for both breathing and burning. He showed that all substances are made up of elements – and not a mixture of earth, air, fire and water, which is what people had believed since ancient times. Boyle is often called the father of modern chemistry.

SOURCE C: *John Locke's views would turn out to be very influential to people in America and France over the next 100 years – when they got rid of their rulers!*

1686

In London, Isaac Newton discovered that a force (which we call gravity) pulls an object towards the ground. He realized that gravity is what keeps the moon moving around the Earth. He also improved the design of the telescope, wrote a famous book commonly called *Principia*, which helped scientists all over the world understand the universe, and used a prism to show the seven colours of the spectrum. His experiment with light is still done today in science classrooms all over the world.

1662

The Royal Society was formed, backed by King Charles II. This group of scientists met regularly to discuss their ideas and experiments. Charles even increased the number of hanged criminals whose bodies were made available to doctors. This was the first group of its kind in the world and it still meets regularly today. Leading members included Robert Boyle, Samuel Pepys, Sir Isaac Newton and Sir Christopher Wren.

1690

John Locke, an Englishman, wrote many books and essays about the human mind. He said that at birth a human's mind was empty and it was their experiences in life than made them who they were and that good education is very important. He also said that the rulers of any country should work for the benefit of everyone… and if they didn't, the people should get rid of them.

1700

1705

Astronomer Edmond Halley published a report stating that comet sightings in 1456, 1531, 1607 and 1682 related to the same comet. He predicted the comet's return in 1758 and when it was seen again it was called 'Halley's Comet'. The comet continued to appear every 75 or 76 years. It last appeared in 1986 and it is next due to appear in the summer of 2061.

1717

Lady Mary Wortley Montagu experimented with smallpox **inoculations** (a way of preventing a person getting the disease). After the success of her experiments, King George I even had his own grandchildren inoculated!

The Middle Ages – a time when most people believed completely (and without question) in whatever the Church said and that God controlled everything – are often called **the Age of Faith**. The period after this, in the 1600s and 1700s, is often called **the Age of Reason** because it was a time when people observed and explored the world around them and tried new theories and experiments. Some people said that during this time many became better informed, aware of the world and enlightened. This period is also called the **Enlightenment**.

Step 3

Now it's time to meet Robert, a gentleman who lived around the time George II (the son of George I) became king in 1727. Discuss with a partner the answers to the questions around him.

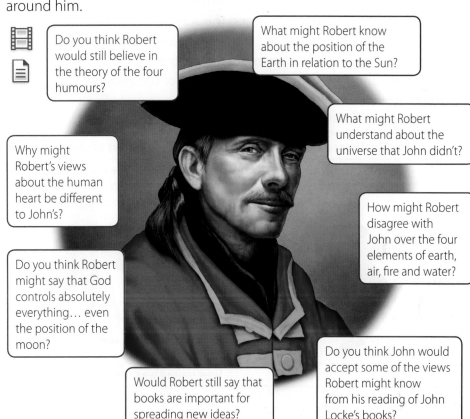

Do you think Robert would still believe in the theory of the four humours?

What might Robert know about the position of the Earth in relation to the Sun?

Why might Robert's views about the human heart be different to John's?

What might Robert understand about the universe that John didn't?

Do you think Robert might say that God controls absolutely everything… even the position of the moon?

How might Robert disagree with John over the four elements of earth, air, fire and water?

Would Robert still say that books are important for spreading new ideas?

Do you think John would accept some of the views Robert might know from his reading of John Locke's books?

Be a Top Historian

Top historians know that, at any one time, there are usually things that are **changing** and things that are **staying the same**. Some changes happen quickly and can be triggered by the publication of a book or essay, for example… but other changes happen slowly, especially if things have been done the same way for thousands of years.

Work

1 **a** Write down five things that John might think about the universe, science and medicine.

   b For each thing, say whether someone living 250 years later (such as Robert) would still think the same or whether they'd think differently. Write in full sentences and explain yourself clearly.

   c Do *you* think we know all there is to know? Or are there lots of things we don't understand about the universe, science and medicine? Explain your answer.

2 **a** Choose three developments or inventions from these pages and explain how they made people healthier.

   b Choose another three developments or inventions and explain how they helped improve people's understanding of the world.

3 **a** Why do you think the Middle Ages are sometimes called the Age of Faith?

   b The time after this is sometimes called the Age of Reason or the Enlightenment. Do you think these are suitable names? Explain your answer.

This book covers the years 1509 to 1745. During this time, some amazing and lasting changes took place. New ideas and discoveries altered the way people looked at the world, whilst new inventions changed the way people did things. Read this section carefully. It doesn't feature all the changes, discoveries and inventions that took place between 1509 and 1745 but it picks out some of the most important and interesting ones.

Mission Objectives

- Judge how far Britain changed between 1509 and 1745.
- Recall at least five important ideas and inventions that came from this time.

1509 The Tudor period	1603 – When Tudors became Stuarts	1745 Georgian period had begun
The relationship between the monarchy and Parliament		

How united was the United Kingdom?		
Two kings, one for England, one for Scotland, different Parliaments; the English king controlled Wales and large parts of Ireland too 	King of England is also King of Scotland with different Parliaments; he still controls Wales and large parts of Ireland 	One king, one Parliament for England, Scotland, and Wales; Ireland's Parliament is under English control! 
How many people?		

England 2.25 million, Wales 0.2 million, Scotland 0.5 million, Ireland 0.8 million; **Total = 3.75 million**	England 4–5 million; Ireland, Scotland and Wales made up a further 2 million of Britain's overall population; **Total = 6–7 million**	England and Wales 6.25 million, Scotland 1.25 million, Ireland 3.25 million, British settlers overseas 3.0 million; **Total = 13.75 million** (including 3 million living abroad)

1509	1603	1745

How many large towns and cities?

Towns and cities with over 2000 inhabitants 	Towns and cities with over 2000 inhabitants 	Towns and cities with over 2000 inhabitants 

What about religion?

 Everyone Catholic	Most people are Church of England (Protestant); Catholics are persecuted 	Most people are Church of England (Protestant); other religions are supposed to be free, but some restrictions still apply!

The main types of communication

 Mainly word of mouth	 Printed books and some newspapers (called broadsheets) are available but expensive	 Newspapers and magazines more common

How did people get around?

The rich travelled by horse (and carriage), the poor walked 	Richer men and women still travelled by horse and carriage – and the poor still walked	Still horses and carriages and walking! There were sedan chairs (an early type of taxi) in the towns, though 

The main types of food and drink

 Beer, wine, cheese, meat, bread, vegetables, knives and spoons	 Beer, wine, cheese, meat, bread, more vegetables, salad, tobacco, knives and spoons	 Beer, wine, tea, coffee, drinking chocolate, cheese, meat, bread, more vegetables, potatoes, bananas, coconuts, salad, tobacco, knives, forks and spoons

A changing nation

1509	1603	1745
What places did Europeans know about?		

Popular entertainment		
 Hunting, jousting (for the rich), fighting games and blood sports; the poor liked a good drink at the local inn or tavern (pub) too	 Going to the theatre, blood sports and mob football; the poor still liked a good drink at the local inn or tavern	 Horse racing, cricket, blood sports and mob football; the poor *still* liked a good drink at the local inn or tavern!
Science and medicine		
 The Earth is the centre of the universe and God holds the answer to everything. Very little is known about science or the human body	 More understanding of Earth's place in the universe; better knowledge of the human body due to more accurate drawings; improved treatment of war wounds	 Lots more is known about chemistry, physics, biology and the universe; it didn't really help people live longer but did bring about new ways of thinking
Law and order		
 Stocks, pillory, whipping and execution are common – but fines remain the most popular type of punishment; no police force	 Older forms of punishment still used. Torture is commonly used to get confessions; witch-hunting becomes a craze! No police force	 Savage punishments and many executions; prisons used more for punishment as well; still no police force!

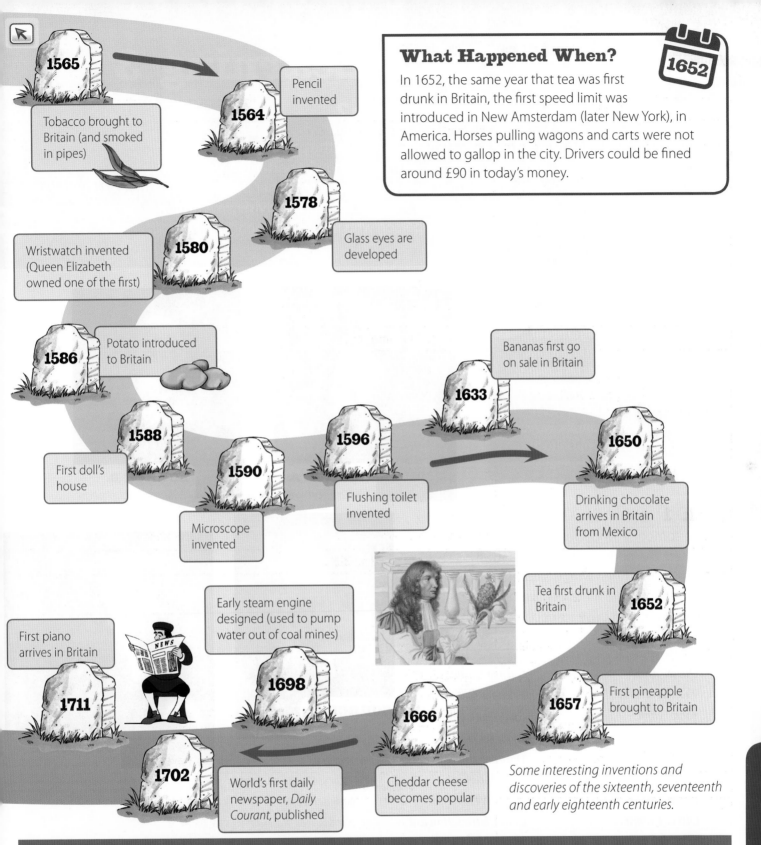

1565

1564 Pencil invented

Tobacco brought to Britain (and smoked in pipes)

1578

Glass eyes are developed

Wristwatch invented (Queen Elizabeth owned one of the first)

1580

1586 Potato introduced to Britain

Bananas first go on sale in Britain

1633

1650

1588 First doll's house

1590 Microscope invented

1596 Flushing toilet invented

Drinking chocolate arrives in Britain from Mexico

Tea first drunk in Britain 1652

First piano arrives in Britain

Early steam engine designed (used to pump water out of coal mines)

1698

1711

1666 Cheddar cheese becomes popular

1657 First pineapple brought to Britain

1702 World's first daily newspaper, *Daily Courant*, published

Some interesting inventions and discoveries of the sixteenth, seventeenth and early eighteenth centuries.

What Happened When? 1652

In 1652, the same year that tea was first drunk in Britain, the first speed limit was introduced in New Amsterdam (later New York), in America. Horses pulling wagons and carts were not allowed to gallop in the city. Drivers could be fined around £90 in today's money.

Work

1 Produce a table with three columns. In the first column, list at least eight key areas (for example, 'law and order' or 'religion'). The second column should be labelled, 'Britain in 1509' and the third, 'Britain in 1745'. Make brief notes about each key area for both of these years.

2 In your opinion, what changed the most, and the least, between 1509 and 1745? Give reasons for your choices.

Assessing Your Learning 3

Why should we remember them?

Good historians are able to work out why some people from the past are important. In fact, historians sometimes use the word 'significant' rather than 'important'. A significant person is someone who has done things that have greatly affected other people's lives – in a good way or a bad way. They might have been a king or queen, an adviser, inventor or explorer, a painter or writer, or just an ordinary person who made a difference!

Be a Top Historian

Remember – being **significant** is *not* the same as being famous. Significant people *can* be famous (but are not always), but famous people are *not* always significant! In today's world, for example, we can all name famous people who have not changed people's lives at all!

SOURCE A:
Oliver Cromwell.

SOURCE B:
William Shakespeare.

Task 1

Choose someone who lived during, or greatly influenced, the period you are currently studying (1509–1745) who is significant or worth remembering. There are a few examples here, but you may want to choose someone different.

SOURCE C:
Henry VIII.

SOURCE D: *Sir Christopher Wren.*

Queen Anne	Galileo Galilei	
Francis Bacon	William Gilbert	
John Cabot	Lady Jane Grey	
William Caxton	Edmond Halley	
Charles I	William Harvey	Mary II
Charles II	John Hawkins	Mary, Queen of Scots
Christopher Columbus	Henry VIII	Samuel Pepys
Oliver Cromwell	Lord Charles Howard	Sir Walter Raleigh
Vasco da Gama	James I and VI	William Shakespeare
Leonardo da Vinci	James II	William Tyndale
Sir Francis Drake	Martin Luther	Antoni van Leeuwenhoek
Edward VI	Ferdinand Magellan	William III
Elizabeth I	Mary I	Sir Christopher Wren

Task 2

Now it's time for you to carry out some research. You might do that by looking through this book or by visiting a library or searching online.

Task 3

Now put together a presentation. This could be done as an essay, a leaflet or even a PowerPoint presentation. Your presentation must:

- Have the title, 'Why is (your chosen person's name) worth remembering?'
- Include basic factual information about their lives, such as when and where they were born and their key jobs, roles and beliefs.
- Describe different events in their lives and their achievements and successes (and failures too, perhaps).
- Give your opinion as to why your chosen person should be remembered today. What did they do that was significant? How did they change lots of people's lives? Did they make short- or long-term changes – or both?

Assessing your work

Look at the success criteria for this task to help you plan and evaluate your work.

Be a Top Historian

Be careful when searching online. Don't just go to one website and get all your information there. Use a variety of websites and also use evidence from books to build up a picture of your chosen person. Try websites like bbc.co.uk and oxfordreference.com to start with.

SOURCE E: *Elizabeth I.*

Hungry for More?

Research a famous historical figure from this period in time who is NOT one of the choices listed on page 152. Write a letter to your teacher arguing why he or she should be included as one of the period's most significant people.

Good	In a good **good** presentation, you would…	• provide a basic outline of the person's life • use dates and historical terms correctly • explain why the person was important or significant • have started to produce structured work.
Better	In a good **better** presentation, you would…	• provide an outline of the person's life, including accurate dates and historical terms • select and use information to explain why the person was significant, using correct historical terms • produce properly structured work.
Best	In the **best** presentation, you would…	• provide an accurate outline of the person's life • explain in detail why the person should be remembered and how their actions and achievements changed lots of people's lives, mentioning short- or long-term changes, or both • show how you made your decisions about what was significant about the person's life • select, organize and use relevant information, using the correct historical terms to produce structured work • show where you got your information from.

Glossary

Act of Settlement An act passed by Parliament stating that after Queen Anne's death the throne would pass to the nearest Protestant heir

Act of Union An act passed by Parliament to unite England, Scotland and Wales under the control of one parliament, based in London

Age of Faith The Middle Ages, when most people believed unquestioningly in the Church and God

Age of Reason Also known as the Enlightenment, the period during the 1600s and 1700s when people began to explore the world more and make new discoveries

Ally A group on the same side as another in battle

Antibiotic A chemical substance used to destroy bacteria

Anti-Stratfordian Someone who doubts that Shakespeare really wrote the plays attributed to him

Architect A designer of buildings

Armada A fleet of warships

Astrolabe A piece of navigation equipment that helped sailors work out how far north or south they were whilst at sea

Astronomer A person who scientifically studies stars, planets and other bodies of the universe

Beacon A fire set in a high place as a warning or signal

Belladonna A chemical used by Tudor women to make their eyes shine and sparkle

Bias To be for or against a person or group of people, especially in a way that is considered unfair

Bill of Mortality A weekly list of the causes of death in a particular place

Bill of Rights The agreements made between William and Mary and Parliament in 1689

Birch A bundle of twigs tied together and used to hit children as a punishment; a cane was a single piece of wood

Blood sports Sports that involve the wounding or killing of animals

Bloodletting The practice of making someone bleed to cure an illness

Bubonic A type of plague that causes huge, round boils or 'buboes'; carried by fleas

Canting A secretive street language used by sturdy beggars

Catholic A follower of Catholicism, one of the main Christian religions

Cavalier Nickname for a soldier who fought for the king during the English Civil War

Cavalry Soldiers on horseback

Citizen A person who lives in a town

Civil war A war between two groups of people in the same country

Class A group of people with the same economic or social status

Cochineal A red dye or colouring obtained from insects

Colony An area of land in a new country occupied by people who still remain under the rule of their homeland

Commonwealth An independent state or community without a monarch

Consummate To make a marriage legally recognised by having sex

Contemporary Something from the same period of time

Crescent A curved, moon-like shape

Cuckold The name for a married person whose husband or wife was having affairs behind their back

Cudgels A game for two people; each person has a heavy stick and they take it in turns to hit each other; the person left standing is the winner

Death warrant A piece of paper ordering someone's execution

Desolation Complete emptiness or destruction

Dissolution The act of officially breaking up an organization; used to describe the time when Henry VIII closed all the monasteries in England and Wales

Divine Right of Kings The belief that kings and queens could do as they wished because they were appointed by God

Ducking stool A punishment for 'unruly' wives

Enlightenment See **Age of Reason**

Excommunicate To expel from the Catholic Church; a very serious punishment

Execution The process of killing or beheading an enemy or convicted criminal

Extremist A supporter of extreme measures (often political or religious)

Familiar A demon, in the form of an animal, that accompanies a witch

Fire mark Displayed on the outside of people's houses to prove that their insurance fees had been paid

Forbade When someone has not allowed something to happen

Galleon A large warship

Gallery A place to sit in a theatre

Gangrene The death of tissues in the body caused by an infection or obstruction of blood flow

Gentleman Rich men, often dukes, earls or lords; they often own a lot of land

Grammar school A school that taught mainly Latin and Greek grammar

Gun-port An opening in a ship through which a gun can be fired

Heathen A person who has no religion or whose religion is not the same as that of another group of people

Hornbook A flat, double-sided paddle, shaped like a table-tennis bat; used to help students read and write

House of Correction Criminals and people who refused to work were sent here; they were forced to make things that were later sold

Imported Brought in from another country, usually by boat

Independent Free from the control of someone or something

Indulgences You could 'buy' these from a bishop; they helped a person pass through purgatory more quickly

Infantry Soldiers on foot

Infidel See **Heathen**

Inoculation A way of preventing a person getting a disease by introducing a small amount of it into their body, making them immune to it

Interregnum The period from the execution of Charles I in 1649 to when Charles II became king; when Oliver Cromwell ruled as Lord Protector

Labourer A person who does manual work such as working in the fields

Laxative A medicine used to help a person go to the toilet easily

Lord Protector The title of the head of state in England between 1653 and 1659, a position first held by Oliver Cromwell

Major-General A man appointed by Cromwell to run one of the 11 districts in England

Malaria A disease spread by mosquitoes

Martyr A person who is prepared to die for their beliefs

Merchant A person whose job is to buy and sell goods in order to make a profit

Mercy Showing understanding or kindness, especially to your enemy

Miscarry When a baby dies while it is still in the womb

Monarch A king or queen

Musket A type of long gun

Musketeer A soldier who carries a musket

Native American The tribesmen who have lived on the continent of North America for thousands of years

Native A member of the original race of a country; a person who was born in that country

Navigation The process of working out where you are

Obituary Briefly tells of some of the most important events, achievements and personality of a person who has recently died

Parliamentarian A supporter of Parliament during the English Civil War

Pauper Someone with no job who relies on charity

Pike A long pole, tipped with a steel spike; used as a weapon

Pikeman A soldier who uses a pike

Pilgrim A person who travels to a place for religious reasons; the first people to colonize America

Pirate A person who attacks and robs ships at sea

Pit The standing area nearest the stage in a theatre

Playwright A person who writes plays

Plundering Taking goods by force

Poor Law A law passed in 1601 that placed paupers into four categories; each group was treated differently

Pope The leader of the Catholic Church, who lives in Rome

Population All the people who live in a particular place

Privateer A sailor who had permission to attack and steal from foreign ships

Propaganda False or misleading information used to spread a certain point of view

Protestants A group of Christians who protested against the Catholic Church

Purgatory The place between heaven and hell; a person is believed to be punished in purgatory for any sins they have committed while alive

Quarter Mercy shown towards an enemy

Quill pen A pen made from a feather; dipped in ink to write

Recusant A Catholic who refused to accept the authority of the Church of England

Reformation The name used to describe the changes or reforms made to the Catholic Church in the sixteenth century, mainly by Henry VIII and his son, King Edward VI

Regicide The official word for killing a king or queen, or for someone who kills a king or queen

Religious Settlement Made by Elizabeth in order to keep the peace between Catholics and Protestants

Renaissance The period between the fourteenth and sixteenth centuries in Europe when there was a rebirth in art, literature and learning

Republic A country without a king or a queen

Restoration The return of a monarch to the throne of England when Charles II became king in 1660

Revolution The overthrowing of a government or social order in favour of a new system

Ridicule To make fun of someone in an unkind way

Roundhead Nickname for Parliament's soldiers during the English Civil War

Routine An established pattern of behaviour that people follow most of the time

Royalist A supporter of the king during the English Civil War

Sash A coloured strip of cloth used to identify soldiers in battle

Scold's bridle An iron mask put over a woman's head to stop her talking; used as a punishment

Searcher Someone who looked for the dead bodies of plague victims during the Great Plague of 1665

Settler Somebody who moved to an area that was previously uninhabited or unknown

Sewer A drain to remove waste water and other rubbish

Shin-hacking A game for two people; each person wears their heaviest boots, they take it in turns to kick each other, and the person left standing is the winner

Ship tax A sum of money, introduced by Charles I, paid by people who were living by the sea

Shorthand A type of coded writing that can be written quickly

Siege A method of attack where an army surrounds a town and threatens to attack unless the town surrenders

Slave A person who is the legal property of someone else and is forced to obey them

Slave trader A person who deals in the transporting and selling of human beings as slaves

Sphere Ball-shaped

Stillborn A baby that is born dead

Stratfordian Someone who believes that Shakespeare was responsible for writing the plays attributed to him

Strolling player A travelling actor, musician and entertainer

Sturdy beggar A criminal who used clever tricks to get money

Superstitious Someone who believes in omens and ghosts

Symptom A sign of an illness or disease

Tithe A type of tax; peasants had to give 10 per cent of their harvest to the priest every year

Treason A crime against a king or queen

Tuberculosis A lung disease

Tyrant A cruel and demanding ruler

Unstable Something that is not secure

Vagabonds Wanderers or tramps

Voyage A journey, usually by sea

Whitsun The seventh Sunday after Easter, also called Pentecost

Wife sale A type of divorce; in Tudor and Stuart England it was possible to sell your wife at one of these

Yeoman A farmer – some were rich; others were poor

Yield Surrender

Index

NOTES TO HELP YOU USE THIS INDEX:

Kings, queens and other royals are listed by their first name, so look for 'Henry VIII' and not 'King Henry VIII'. All other people are listed by their surname, so look for 'Boleyn, Anne' and not 'Anne Boleyn'.

UNIVERSITY PRESS

Great Clarendon Street, Oxford, OX2 6DP, United Kingdom

Oxford University Press is a department of the University of Oxford.
It furthers the University's objective of excellence in research,
scholarship, and education by publishing worldwide. Oxford is a
registered trade mark of Oxford University Press in the UK and in
certain other countries

British Library Cataloguing in Publication Data
Data available

978-0-19-839320-7

10 9 8 7 6

Paper used in the production of this book is a natural, recyclable
product made from wood grown in sustainable forests.
The manufacturing process conforms to the environmental
regulations of the country of origin.

Printed in India by Manipal Technologies Ltd

Acknowledgements

The publishers would like to thank the following for permissions to use their photographs:

p.10: Mary Evans Picture Library; **p.10-11:** Hatfield House, Hertfordshire, UK / The Bridgeman Art Library; **p.12:** National Portrait Gallery; **p.13:** Stock Shots / Alamy; **p.16:** National Portrait Gallery; **p.16:** National Portrait Gallery; **p.17:** Bridgeman Art Library/ Kunsthistorisches Museum Vienna; **p.17:** Bridgeman Art Library/ Musee de Louvre; **p.17:** The Royal Collection/ 2008 HM Queen Elizabeth II; **p.19:** Bristol City Museum and Art Gallery, UK / The Bridgeman Art Library; **p.19:** The Bridgeman Art Library; **p.20:** Illustrated London News Ltd/Mary Evans; **p.21:** Jeanne Mcright/ Dreamstime.com; **p.21:** Steven Vidler/Corbis; **p.22:** The Royal Collection /2008 HM Queen Elizabeth II; **p.24:** National Portrait Gallery; **p.25:** The Stapleton Collection / The Bridgeman Art Library; **p.26-27:** Bridgeman Art Library/Trustees of the Bedford Estate, Woburn Abbey; **p.29:** With kind permission of Harvington Hall, Kidderminster www.harvingtonhall.com; **p.34:** REX/Universal History Archive / Universal Images Group; **p.35:** The Granger Collection/ TopFoto; **p.35:** The Print Collector / Alamy; **p.36:** British Library, Shelfmark/Man; **p.36:** The Art Gallery Collection / Alamy; **p.37:** INTERFOTO / Sammlung Rauch / Mary Evans; **p.38:** GL Archive / Alamy; **p.41:** Frank Bach/Shutterstock; **p.41:** National Trust Photo Library/ Derek Croucher; **p.41:** National Trust Photo Library/John Miller; **p.41:** Scottish Viewpoint Picture Library; **p.42:** Staatliche Museen, Berlin, Germany / Bildarchiv Foto Marburg / The Bridgeman Art Library; **p.42:** Fotomas / TopFoto; **p.42:** National Maritime Museum, Greenwich, London; **p.42:** Tomas Abad / Alamy; **p.47:** The Stapleton Collection / The Bridgeman Art Library; **p.48:** The Art Archive / Alamy; **p.50:** Mary Evans Picture Library; **p.51:** National Portrait Gallery, London; **p.53:** Peter Phipp/Getty Images; **p.59:** TopFoto / Fotomas; **p.61:** TopFoto / Fotomas; **p.65:** Image Asset Management Ltd. / Alamy; **p.66:** SMaloney; **p.73:** Her Majesty Queen Elizabeth II / The Bridgeman Art Library; **p.74:** Burghley House Collection, Lincolnshire, UK / The Bridgeman Art Library; **p.74:** Mary Evans Picture Library; **p.74:** Woburn Abbey, Bedfordshire, UK / The Bridgeman Art Library; **p.75:** Ken Welsh / The Bridgeman Art Library; **p.75:** National Portrait Gallery, London; **p.77:** Mary Evans Picture Library; **p.79:** Worthing Museum and Art Gallery, Sussex, UK / The Bridgeman Art Library; **p.84:** Mary Evans Picture Library; **p.85:** Topfoto/Fotomas; **p.86:** Mary Evans Picture Library; **p.87:** National Portrait Gallery, London; **p.88:** Mary Evans Picture Library; **p.90:** Mary Evans Picture Library; **p.91:** The Granger Collection / TopFoto; **p.91:** Wellcome Library, London; **p.100:** Private Collection / The Bridgeman Art Librar; **p.101:** Topham / Fotomas; **p.101:** Topham / Fotomas; **p.104:** The Art Archive/Alamy; **p.106-7:** Houses of Parliament, Westminster, London, UK / The Bridgeman Art Library; **p.107:** Ashmolean Museum, University of Oxford, UK / The Bridgeman Art Library; **p.109:** British Library Board/ The Bridgeman Art Library; **p.109:** The Art Gallery Collection/Alamy; **p.110:** Heritage Images/Corbis; **p.111:** Brooklyn Museum/Corbis; **p.113:** Mary Evans Picture Library; **p.114:** Corbis/Martin Jones; **p.116:** Private Collection / The Bridgeman Art Library; **p.118:** National Portrait Gallery, London; **p.119:** National Archives; **p.119:** Doctorpete; **p.120:** Mary Evans Picture Library/GROSVENOR PRINTS; **p.120:** Museum of London, UK / The Bridgeman Art Library; **p.121:** Mary Evans Picture Library; **p.122:** Image Asset Management Ltd. / Alamy; **p.123:** Wellcome Library, London; **p.127:** Museum of Fine Arts, Budapest, Hungary / The Bridgeman Art Library; **p.127:** Topfoto/Corporation of London/HIP; **p.128:** Michael Nicholson/Corbis; **p.130:** National Portrait Gallery, London; **p.130:** Nick Turner / Alamy; **p.131:** Dan Breckwoldt /Shutterstock; **p.131:** Mary Evans Picture Library; **p.133:** TopFoto/Fortean; **p.137:** Christie's Images / The Bridgeman Art Library; **p.138:** The Print Collector/Corbis; **p.139:** Timothy Millett Collection / The Bridgeman Art Library; **p.140:** Getty Images; **p.141:** GL Archive / Alamy; **p.141:** GL Archive / Alamy; **p.143:** Private Collection / The Bridgeman Art Library; **p.143:** The Royal Collection Picture Library; **p.145:** Bettman/Corbis; **p.145:** Mary Evans Picture Library; **p.145:** World History Archive/TopFoto; **p.146:** Bettman/ Corbis; **p.146:** Mary Evans/Iberfoto; **p.146:** Sue Sharp

Cover illustration by Matthew Hollings

Illustrations by Moreno Chiacchiera, Jamil Dar, Rudolf Farkas, Tony Randell, Martin Sanders, Clive Wakfer and Gareth Clarke

We are grateful to Independent Talent and the BBC for permission to reprint the comment by Fiona Shaw on her programme Great Britons: William Shakespeare, BBC, November 2002.

We have made every effort to trace and contact all copyright holders before publication, but if notified of any errors or omissions, the publisher will be happy to rectify these at the earliest opportunity.

From the author, Aaron Wilkes: The author wishes to again thank the brilliant Humanities team at OUP for their energy, enthusiasm and support during the preparation of this book. A huge thank you in particular must go to my publisher, Sarah Flynn, and my editor, Becky DeLozier, who have worked tirelessly on this project and have never once moaned when I've sent them an email or texted them late into the evening. Their kind words of encouragement and their 'can do' attitude make them an absolute pleasure to work with. I would also like to acknowledge Janice Chan, Lois Durrant, Laura Syred and Fiona MacColl at OUP for their hard work. I must also thank my ever supportive and patient wife, Emma, and my very understanding daughters, Hannah and Eleanor, who have never once complained when I've diverted our car journey to go and look at a castle ruin or an obscure seventeenth-century town house!

The publishers would like to thank the following people for offering their contribution in the development of this book and related components:
James Ball, for writing parts of the Second Editions of the books in this series.
Patrick Taylor, Director of Teaching at Chenderit School, for literacy consultancy.
Jerome Freeman, Educational Consultant, for assessment consultancy.

Links to third party websites are provided by Oxford in good faith and for information only. Oxford disclaims any responsibility for the materials contained in any third party website referenced in this work.